THE
PURPOSE
HANDBOOK

A beginner's guide to figuring out what
you're here to do

ELOISE SKINNER

First published in Great Britain by Practical Inspiration
Publishing, 2021

© Eloise Skinner, 2021

The moral rights of the author have been asserted

ISBN   9781788602846   (print)
        9781788602839   (epub)
        9781788602822   (mobi)

TABLE OF CONTENTS

PREFACE

"Be patient toward all that is unsolved in your heart and try to love the questions themselves like locked rooms and like books that are written in a very foreign tongue. Do not now seek the answers, which cannot be given you because you would not be able to live them. And the point is, to live everything. Live the questions now. Perhaps you will then gradually, without noticing it, live along some distant day into the answer."

Rilke (*Letters to a Young Poet*)

In support of Career Ready UK

Career Ready is a national charity with a mission to boost social mobility by empowering young people and giving their talents a platform to flourish (check out the Resources chapter of this book for some more information and background). A portion of the proceeds of this book will be donated to Career Ready.

ABOUT THIS BOOK: AN INTRODUCTION

If someone asked you about your purpose, what would you say?

Think about your goals; your ambitions. Think about what drives you, about who you are and what you're trying to do in the world. What's your purpose? Would you know how to answer the question?

It's strange, because it seems like such a fundamentally important subject, and yet most of us probably don't have an immediate, clear response. We feel like we know ourselves and our everyday actions intimately – and we do, of course – but we often forget to step back for a moment and really look at our lives. It's possible that we spend more time curating our social media feeds than we do our actual existence.

We live in a rapidly changing world. The traditional paths of our parents' and grandparents' generations have lost their power. The authority and structures of religion can seem outdated. Mostly, we get to define our own lives now – whether we get married, have children, move to the other side of the world

– but we're left without guidance in the process. Often, even when we get what we were working towards, we end up wondering – what was the point? What was it that I was looking for? Do I have a particular purpose here? Does any of this actually matter?

This story is familiar to me, because – for a long time – it was my story. After university, I attempted the typical millennial journey: degree, city career, responsibilities, social life, five-year plan. I always imagined a sense of purpose would fall into place without too much effort. I guess I thought that matching my life up to traditional signs of achievement would reward me with the deeper meaning I'd been looking for. Spoiler alert: it didn't. I felt almost betrayed by this outcome – like I'd been promised something, and when I'd worked to achieve it, it didn't deliver.

And so, I went searching for purpose. I looked for it in job opportunities and charity projects and meditation retreats. I qualified as a yoga teacher and moved to another country. I even spent a year training to be a monk (more on that later). Gradually, I started to gather together purpose-finding practices and tools that, over a long period of time, I used to design a personal sense of purpose, passion and intention.

The beauty of these kinds of purpose-finding practices is that you don't have to become a monk to claim them for yourself. You don't have to spend hours studying, or learn a specific technique, or follow a certain set of rules with perfection. Instead, you can integrate purpose-finding practices into your current life just as it is, bringing with you everything that you have – including the whole of your past, as well as your hopes and dreams for the future. And that's where this book comes in.

This book doesn't tell you precisely *what* to think about the topic of purpose, and it doesn't instruct you *how* to approach it. It's not promising to fix your life. Instead, think of this book as your guide as you navigate the questions of meaning and purpose for yourself. Part manifesto, part manual, this book will walk you through the reasons why developing a sense of purpose is so important, and will give you a number of practical strategies as you begin to navigate your own path. There are also sections covering the practical aspects of this work, and a chapter dedicated to supporting your journey with some overall wellness tools.

As you start to develop your purpose-finding practices, you'll discover that this work is deeply integrated with everything else in your life. This is not a career book, but you might find that your career progresses with more success. This is not a relationship book, but you might find that your relationships start to go deeper and carry more integrity. This is not a wellness book, but you might find that your own sense of personal wellbeing is better than it ever has been. Once you begin, this work starts to expand; eventually, it touches every part of your life. After all, this work is about the most fundamental questions you can ask yourself – who you are, and what you're doing in the world.

The path towards finding your purpose isn't designed to make you into some kind of mission-driven machine, or to give you a singular focus to pursue for the rest of your life. This book is about something much more interesting – the idea that it's possible to experience your life one level deeper than the life you've experienced so far. It's about choosing to create a life infused with intention, integrity and meaning. Fundamentally, this book is centred around the idea that it's possible to *design* the life you actually want to live – to be a creator, rather than an observer.

The journey of finding your purpose will, of course, look different for everyone – but this book provides a portfolio of resources to get started. I encourage you to approach the book like a toolkit: full of suggestions and advice, ready for you to try out in practice. See what works; see what doesn't. Add your own suggestions in the margins. Work through it, highlight what you love and revisit it regularly. Take ownership of the process: it's your life, after all.

While I was writing this book, I had a conversation with a mentor about my own career ambitions. He mentioned, in passing, that very few people are fortunate enough to figure out their purpose in life. If that's true, it's time to create change. I want you to be part of that change, and my hope is that the work of this book serves as an introduction.

A final note, before we get started. This isn't a sprint – this is more like a steady trek. When I was on my monastic training, we were often encouraged to think of the programme as a pilgrimage, and I find that to be a helpful metaphor when it comes to starting the purpose-finding path. A pilgrimage is slow, steady and intentional. The steps aren't taken to prove something to others, but to discover something about yourself – who you are, and what you're contributing to the world. This is a lifelong journey, and there's no finish line: the work is always ongoing. But it's important work. In fact, it might just be the most important work you ever do.

BEFORE YOU START

Gather your materials

In order to complete the exercises in this book, it will be helpful to have a dedicated notebook. It doesn't have to be anything special, just something you can refer back to – and perhaps something you can keep for the years to come, as you develop this work over time.

There is also a **free** PDF workbook, downloadable from www.thepurposeworkshop.uk/resources, which you can use to guide you through some of the main exercises. The pencil symbol below will show you where there's a corresponding section in the PDF workbook:

The structure of the book

1. Chapters 1 and 2 are your introduction to the topic. We get started with a couple of small exercises and set up the foundations for the work ahead.

2. Chapters 3 and 4 are your major purpose-focused exercises. Feel free to take your time with these, and mark your favourites to return to periodically.

3. Chapters 5, 6 and 7 are your support-ing framework. This is where we'll step

outside the specific question of 'finding purpose' and look at the topic in a more holistic, integrated way.

4. Chapter 8 contains the purpose-focused questions I've been asked hundreds of times, and Chapter 9 is a collection of case studies and profiles of those who have inspired me on my own purpose-focused path. This chapter is a great example of the diversity of approaches to purpose.

5. And then, to finish up – some resources for you, and a couple of extra suggestions, exercises and next steps.

My general approach

The approach of this book is (I hope!) open, inviting and welcoming. As your guide, I see myself as walking alongside you through this work, rather than telling you exactly what to do. And so, the exercises are offerings, and you're free to adapt and amend them to suit your own lifestyle. At the same time, I want you to dive in: try things out, commit to doing the work, and see what happens. I've experienced the power of purpose-focused work in many people's lives (including my own!), and I hope you'll trust the process.

Okay – that's all. Let's begin.

Chapter 1

THE TOPIC OF PURPOSE

What it's all about, and three initial exercises

Purpose: 'the reason for which something is done or created or for which something exists'.

Sounds pretty fundamental, doesn't it? It's a topic that goes to the heart of our existence as humans, but one that's easy to forget beneath the daily chaos of emails, meetings and our ever-expanding to-do lists. But it might just be amongst the most fundamental questions we ever encounter. In this chapter, we'll start with why the concept of purpose matters, and move on to how you can start to think about it with more clarity.

The purpose of purpose

It's worth noting that this is not a new question. Although it's often reported that the next generation will demand 'purpose-driven lives', the concept of purpose wasn't invented alongside avocado toast and Instagram. This topic, and the questions that accompany it, have been around for a long time. In fact, people have been asking themselves – and each other – about the idea of purpose for thousands of years.

This might remove some of the novelty from the discussion, but it makes it a little more exciting. It means that you're about to become part of a tradition of people who've asked the same questions, and who have started to walk the same path. In some ways, the search for purpose connects us to countless numbers of people, at a level of depth and continuity that we don't often experience.

At the same time, however, the question is completely new for each individual, and the work of finding your purpose is utterly unique. In the past, people might have sought purpose through social organizations, family structures or religious communities (and many still do). And, of course, if those paths deliver the structure and the answers you're searching for, that's great. This book is not an alternative to any of that – it can be an addition.

For those of us searching for purpose outside those structures, the same types of 'life questions' are still relevant – this, after all, is the work of being a thinking, feeling human being. And as you might be starting to recognize, very few people actually do the difficult work of thinking about these life questions in a deliberate, consistent way.

In terms of the evidence, research has started to show what we've all long suspected: finding purpose in your work life might make you happier, more energized and more fulfilled.[1] Recent research also indicates that a sense of passion is an essential component of grit.[2] And the benefits of finding purpose aren't limited to your working hours: research suggests that people who demonstrate a sense of purpose in their lives have a lowered mortality risk.[3]

Aside from the statistics, though – how can it help you? Practically, what's the point of putting time and effort into this work? Here are a few suggestions to start with.

Purpose can become a guide

Life is complex. Throughout your hours on earth, you'll be thrown a multitude of challenges. How

---

[1] For example: www.forbes.com/sites/rodgerdeanduncan/ 2018/09/11/the-why-of-work-purpose-and-meaning-really-do-matter/#6ab48ebd68e1

[2] www.pnas.org/content/115/40/9980

[3] https://journals.sagepub.com/doi/abs/10.1177/0956 797614531799

will you know which way to turn? Those driven by purpose will have a clearer sense of the road ahead. It doesn't guarantee an easy journey, but it can help to keep you on your path. Purpose can operate as a personal compass, pointing you in the right direction when you reach a place of uncertainty. On a day-to-day level, this can help in making decisions, choosing between options or articulating your values.

Purpose inspires others

What would it be like if everyone – from your boss, to your barista, to the tube driver who gets you to work – was driven by a sense of purpose? What if we all woke up in the morning knowing that our work is aligned with a deeper sense of who we are? Chances are, things would look a little different to the way they appear now. A purpose-orientated world would probably be more energized, more vibrant, and more inspired. And on a personal level, the journey to living a purpose-focused life might be slow, but you're likely to carry others with you along the way. Whether you're aware of it or not, you're modelling a lifestyle to everyone you encounter: if your template is purpose-driven, it might just become an example for someone else to follow.

Think about your heroes, too – the people you look up to in your career, or the people who inspire you in your daily life. It's likely that they have at least one thing in common: a resilient sense of who they are and an idea of what they want to contribute to the world. This is what often attracts us to strong characters: the way they move through their lives with a feeling of intention, meeting challenges and obstacles with determination. This quality doesn't have to be reserved for heroes and inspirational figures and people we look up to. A purpose-focused life is available to each and every one of us.

Purpose gives rise to grit

Grit: the blend of passion and perseverance that helps you power through the ups, downs, disappointments and difficulties of life. 'Grit' (a term developed and researched by academic and psychologist Angela Duckworth and colleagues) is often established when its owner has a clear idea of what it is they're fighting for. And while it might be true that some people are more predisposed to this kind of attitude than others, it can be practised, learned and experienced by anyone. Figuring out your sense of purpose is one route to getting there.

A note on the use of language

You've probably heard the words 'purpose', 'mission' and 'passion' thrown around quite a bit. But what do they actually mean? Are they the same, or different?

Here's a simple guide to knowing what you're talking about, so you can navigate a purpose-focused conversation with ease and excellence.

Purpose

Basic definition: 'purpose is the intention, aim or function of something; the thing that something is supposed to achieve'.

Your purpose is often thought of as the 'thing you're here to do'. You'll have heard people speak about 'finding purpose' or 'searching for purpose'. But an individual's sense of purpose doesn't have to be one singular focus that lasts a lifetime. The concept of purpose is fluid, and will (and probably should) evolve throughout your life. At some points, your primary purpose might be to deliver exceptional value in a new role at work. At other times, your primary purpose might turn your attention to your close relationships, or to a self-development project. It's okay to let your purpose shift as you develop and progress. The key is to become aware of it (much more on awareness later), without forcing yourself into a particular template.

Your purpose might be a long-term idea, or it might be something more immediate. Perhaps it's an overarching goal (for example: giving back to your community) or something more tangible (for example: getting promoted within the next few months).

The specific formulation is less important than the process of figuring it out, since it will be the things you learn in the process that provide the insight into your own life and character. And, of course, the important side-effects: the clarity, focus and drive that the 'figuring-out process' will deliver.

It's also okay not to know what your purpose is for the time being. Not everyone will fall into an immediate awareness of what they want to do in the world. Let the process of working it out be an exploration of your life – stay curious, be patient, keep asking the questions, and let the answers arrive in their own time. In the introduction to this book, we touched on the metaphor of 'pilgrimage' – this is where that idea starts to become helpful. Each piece of purpose-focused work is a step on the journey. If you keep your eyes on the path, rather than gazing into the distance, you might end up further than you had ever imagined.

Mission

Basic definition: 'a mission is an important goal, accompanied by strong conviction'.

Mission and purpose can seem like similar concepts, and they often overlap. Your 'mission', however, is normally a shorter-term project than your 'life purpose'. Your mission might be specific to your particular situation

– it might be a career ambition that you want to achieve within the next few months, or a particular mentoring relationship you want to develop. You might have more than one mission, and your mission might develop into a greater purpose over time.

To help clarify this idea, your mission can often be crystallized in the form of a 'personal mission statement'. This statement can become a helpful guide as you move forwards in your life. A mission statement also carries the benefit of being fairly flexible – you can write and rewrite it as your life evolves, and you can have a couple of mission statements running in parallel (for example: one for work, one for personal projects, and one for family relationships).

You can create your personal mission statement using the following steps:

1. Figure out what your main goal is (could be work-related, personal or relationship-based, depending on what you want to use this mission statement for).
2. Note down how you want to achieve that goal – what kind of character you want to develop in the process; who you want to be on the journey towards your goal.
3. Give yourself a rough estimate of how much time you want to dedicate to the mission.

Here's a simple example, using a career-orientated goal:

Main goal: promotion to next tier of leadership at work

How to achieve: through growing a personal brand as someone who excels at their role

Time estimate: six months

Mission statement: to obtain career promotion over the next six months, using enhanced personal brand and reputation for excellence

We'll revisit the idea of making a mission statement in Chapter 3.

Passion

Basic definition: 'passion is an intense desire or enthusiasm for something'.

This final definition is about your passion – and of course, you can (and probably do!) have more than one. The term can be used in all sorts of ways: sometimes you'll hear it used to describe a lifelong love of something ('music has always been my passion'), and sometimes you'll hear it with reference to something recent ('this new job has become my passion'). It's probably fairly clear to you what your passions are, but you can use the following guiding questions to capture them with more accuracy:

- Start with your interests and hobbies. What do you most love to do? What are you doing when you feel most 'in flow', and lose track of time? When do you feel most focused, engaged and productive?
- If you had unlimited money, what would you do tomorrow?
- If your current job suddenly halved your salary, what would you do tomorrow? Would you still show up for work, or would you pursue another path?
- What did you love most growing up, or when you were younger? What were you best known for – did you have any special skills or talents that you loved to practise?
- What do you most look forward to during your week? Why do you look forward to it? Is it the nature of the activity, or the people you're with, or the way you feel afterwards?

The answers to these questions should give you a sense of where your passions lie – and if you have a long list, you might begin to see similarities between them, or consistent themes that you can pick out. They'll probably feed into, or overlap with, your purpose and your mission, too: that's totally fine – and makes sense, when you think about it. The intention is for all of these pieces to fit together, giving you greater clarity about who you are and where your place is in the world.

The art of reframing

Perhaps you're convinced on the theoretical benefits of a purpose-driven life. But where to begin? Throughout the next few chapters, we'll work through a number of practical exercises to start thinking about your purpose in greater detail. But, as much as the work will be about *discovery*, some of it will also be about *reframing* what's already going on in your life, in order to understand it better. Reframing is about thinking through the reality of your day-to-day existence, to find the depth and direction that exists just beneath the surface. Sometimes, the process of working through purpose-finding exercises will enable you to uncover a deeper sense of purpose that's been there all along.

To get you started on the reframing process, here are a few questions.

1. Who are you helping in the course of your day-to-day life?

Make a list of all the people you help directly: your work clients, your colleagues, your bosses, your family members, your neighbours, your community (and so on).

Once you have the list, start to expand it to encompass a broader circle. Consider people you help by contributing to the overall culture of your workplace, or people you help indirectly by volunteering for responsibilities, or by producing new ideas, working on your art or engaging in a process of creativity. Be generous with the boundaries of this exercise. Anything you do to put something useful, positive or beneficial back into the world counts.

Once you have the expanded list, take a long look through it. Is it possible to see a consistent thread between the types of people you help, and the way in which you help them? (There's no need to come up with any revelations at this point – we're just gathering information to help you map out your life in a little more detail.)

2. Does your dream job have an overarching purpose or mission?

Imagine you could work your dream job. What makes that job different from others? Does it have a particular service – or way of delivering a service – that makes it unique? If you're already in a job that suits you well, think about whether your organization has a mission. Does it resonate with you? Does it give you any insight into why you do the work that you do?

3. Can you find pockets of purpose in your existing routines?

Get creative. Even if you don't see your life and work as delivering a sense of purpose (yet), there are nearly always opportunities to spot pockets of purpose for yourself. What about volunteering projects, or mentoring, or creative expression? Sometimes, even a simple chat with a junior colleague or younger family member can deliver a moment of purpose in an otherwise monotonous day. Again, no need to come to a realization at this point – just note down anything that comes to mind.

After all, we're just getting started.

CHAPTER 2

THE PURPOSE MANIFESTO

Why it matters

The work of crafting your life begins here. But there's a question to get to the heart of first: why are we doing this work in the first place? In this chapter, we'll cover the importance of purpose, the way it can change the way you approach everything, and address some common issues that arise along the way.

The importance of purpose

The human mind is an incredible thing. Although we don't always choose our circumstances, we are constantly presented with opportunities to interpret events, set goals and develop our own character. Think about all the things that happen to us without our consent, desire or participation. Death, illness, global pandemics... it's a lengthy list, and it's not always easy to come to terms with it. But we have the capacity, in any given moment, to decide how to greet the things that come our way. Sure, we're pushed in certain directions, or our plans get destroyed, or our dreams get dismantled before our eyes. But even in the bleakest scenarios, when the worst possible thing we thought could happen *does actually happen*, we still have a choice – the choice to respond as we decide. Perhaps, instead of thinking of ourselves as passive observers of our own existence, we could think of ourselves as designers, with the ability to control the things we can control, and the ability to design our responses to the things we can't control.

The skill, then – and it is a learnable skill, rather than something any of us should expect to naturally occur – is to identify the gap between stimulus (something happening to you) and response (the way we choose to respond), so we can figure out what to do next. Let's take an example. Imagine you have a clear career path in your industry. Let's say you studied at university, trained for a professional qualification and ended up at the start of a long, predictable ladder towards your desired role. But then something happens, something you had no control over (a global pandemic, perhaps?) and you're left without job security or prospects in that particular type of work. What next?

On one interpretation, you have no control here – something came your way that you couldn't avoid, and you're forced to react. Perhaps you feel like you have no other option but to desperately search for another path. Or, you could see it another way. Instead of a predetermined reaction to an unavoidable situation, you could see yourself as being presented with a choice. The original option may no longer be open to you. But you have a multitude of other options, just waiting to be discovered.

This way of thinking takes courage and imagination. For many people (myself included), it's not a natural or instinctive way of seeing things. As humans, we're often reactive beings – wanting to fight or flee a situation, or get back to safety as soon as possible. But those instincts can be harnessed and used to your own advantage. So, in a situation where you're not in immediate danger, you can create a space between stimulus and response (more on how to do that in Chapter 7). Within that space, you can pause, realign with your purpose, and make a decision that follows from that foundation.

A sense of inner purpose delivers freedom, because it cannot be taken away by an outside force. It provides each person – regardless of individual circumstances – with the ability to identify their goals and values, and to choose a path with intention. A strong, grounded sense of purpose also delivers independence. It might even mean, for example, that it's not necessary to enter relationships in order to receive validation or reassurance (whether with other people, or with possessions or behaviours).

In some ways, finding (and maintaining) a sense of purpose could be seen as a fundamental pillar of wellness: a way to ensure life is lived to its fullest, and enjoyed in its highest quality. This could be the journey towards a full, complete human life, and it should be available to everyone. This is not just a theoretical or philosophical discussion, either. Finding a sense of purpose can change the way you navigate your life, in a very practical sense.

How purpose can change the way you live

Let's start with a few examples.

One famous case is the life of psychologist Viktor Frankl, who focused his work on the theme of meaning. Human beings, according to Frankl, are beings who have the freedom to decide what they will be in the next moment. At the heart of Frankl's belief about life is the idea that human beings are entities consisting of mind, body and spirit, and that life *always* contains an opportunity to find meaning, under any circumstances.

This is a particularly pertinent message given the circumstances of Frankl's own life. A long-term prisoner in the concentration camps of Nazi Germany, Frankl witnessed the loss of his entire immediate family (other than his sister). Add to this the loss of all possessions, the brutal inhumanity of life in a concentration camp and the constant threat of death: it would be no surprise if an individual faced with these circumstances abandoned all hope. But Frankl's survival, together with his enduring belief in the meaning of life, is a testament to the power of purpose, and the very practical consequences that belief can have.

At the heart of Frankl's message is this: that *no matter the circumstances*, we have the capacity to transcend our suffering and rise above it. We have the ability to 'choose our attitude in a given set of circumstances', in Frankl's words. And the driving force behind this? A sense of meaning. To quote Nietzsche: 'he who has a *why* to live can bear almost any *how*'.[4]

Frankl discusses other stories in his writing.[5] One of these shows how purpose can work in the opposite direction – to disempower, disarm and disillusion those who lose their sense of meaning. The example he gives is of a fellow inmate in the concentration camps, who reported to Frankl a dream of liberation. The dream informed the inmate that liberation would happen on 30 March. In Frankl's recollection, the date approached and the inmate became increasingly depressed. He became severely ill, contracting a fever

---

[4] As quoted in Viktor Frankl's *Man's Search for Meaning* (1946, Penguin Random House).
[5] Viktor Frankl, *Yes to Life* (2019, Penguin Random House).

around the date of 30 March, and died soon after. Frankl offers the story as an example of the power of the 'inner hold': the inner sense of meaning and purpose that drives us forward. As Frankl describes it, this inmate had lost his sense of personal 'drive', and the subsequent loss of the will to live followed.

These are extreme examples, but the lessons within them have universal power. First, that each human being has the capacity to choose, and retains total authority over their own response to life. Second, that this will – the will that comes from the inner sense of meaning, purpose and authority – can be an incredibly powerful source. Its energy can produce incredible results; its loss can change the course of a life entirely. And third, that learning how to intentionally direct this inner sense of purpose can change the way you live. Understanding yourself on this deeper, existential level gives you the power to decide what happens next.

Linking the theory and the practice

In Chapters 3 and 4, you'll get an opportunity to dive into the most practical aspects of this work: collections of exercises that you can work through, in your own time and in your own way. But these exercises are underpinned by a theoretical background – the idea, as mentioned above, that it's possible to create your own life, and to find your purpose regardless of your external circumstances. This isn't an academic book, but there are academic roots to purpose-finding work. If you're interested in Existential Analysis, existentialism or logotherapy, I've included some reading suggestions in the 'Resources' chapter.

How purpose can evolve over time

If you've ever tried to take up a new habit, routine or practice, you'll probably know this to be true: we can only test what we truly believe by living it out, in a very practical way. In order to find our path, we need to start walking – and we might find, in some circumstances, that we're going in the wrong direction. If we can break down what's really going on here, we can unpick a couple of steps.

First, that you – as a human being in this world – are *complex*. This means that it's not always possible, ahead of time, to predict exactly how you'll respond to changes. Take the example of meditation: let's say you've been enchanted by the latest meditation app and you're determined to start your own practice. You can do all the research you want – listening to podcasts, reading books, asking other meditators – but you won't *really* know your own response to meditation until you start doing it. You might love it, or hate it (or you might experience both, at various points). It's hard to know until you get there. We're

21

complicated people, even if we think of ourselves as pretty predictable.

Second, we're also *integrated* people – one aspect of our life affects all the other aspects of our life. Imagine you take up jogging every day, as a new health-focused resolution. Ahead of time, you might predict changes in your level of fitness, along with an improved mood or better sleep. What is less possible to predict is the impact on everything else. Maybe, after a few weeks, you're not as argumentative, or you find yourself becoming more positive, or more calm. Maybe it reminds you of the beauty of nature and you start to plan your move away from the city. Maybe you meet other runners with a similar passion and form a new friendship group. You get the idea. It's hard to isolate parts of your life and address them separately. Purpose-finding work, like everything else, affects everything else.

And, finally, you're *constantly evolving*. We're not the same people as we were yesterday. We're in a constant cycle of renewal, even if you don't notice it from day to day. We get older. Our values shift. Our perspective broadens. And your purpose-finding work should evolve with you.

Do you remember your first career ambition as a child? Chances are, it's different from what you've ended up doing now – although there might be similarities or consistent elements. Purpose-finding work is similar: there might be ongoing themes and intentions throughout your journey, but any specific answers to purpose-focused questions are likely to change along with you.

So, that's the first step – to acknowledge that you're complex, integrated and evolving. (This is sometimes referred to as… being human.)

Next, you need to develop the sense of awareness that will carry you forwards in your life – the ability to notice when things are shifting around you, and the consequential changes to your character. This is a skill, and it's something that can be developed.

Think about all the people you know who got stuck somewhere along the journey of their life. These are the people who stayed decades in a job they hated, or remained in a relationship that they knew would be damaging in the long term. In some cases, this might be an act of intentional denial, but it also might be a consequence of just 'not realizing'. These people might start off by following a path that seemed like the right one, and wake up a decade later realizing that they never did the continuous work of questioning if it was *still* the right path.

So, noticing when things start to change is a skill. It takes conscious effort to do the work of evaluating your own life. But it doesn't have to feel like work – getting to know yourself can actually be pretty interesting. Here are just a couple of ways to do it (many of which are covered in the following chapters):

1. self-analysis practices, such as journaling, reflections, goal-setting, etc.;
2. talking it through with someone – partner, friend, mentor or therapist;
3. doing some kind of creative work that helps you reflect on your life – dance, music, art, making or building things, creative writing (or any other creative practice you have in your life);
4. mind-focused practices like meditation, mindfulness or breathwork; and/or
5. body-focused practices like yoga, walking or running outside, sports or other physical activities.

None of these practices are likely to deliver answers in isolation, but you might find that the combination of various tools teaches you something about yourself, or starts to show you the reality of your life, character and values.

And – the final step – acting on your awareness. It's one thing to embrace change and learn the reasons behind it. It's another (more challenging) thing to decide to act on it. Acting on change takes courage, commitment and maturity. It might mean closing the door on one chapter in order to open another one. It might mean saying goodbye to people, projects and plans that no longer align with where you're headed. It's difficult work, and not many people want to do it. But sometimes the consequences of not taking any action are actually more threatening than the consequences of taking action. Because the consequences of not taking action – even if you can't immediately see them play out – are that you remain in the same place, unable to respond to the direction in which your life is leading you. And if that sounds like something you want to avoid, this book is a good starting point.

Handling your ambition

Ambition has an interesting reputation. If you're part of the Instagram generation, you've probably seen the reclaiming of the word 'ambition' in inspirational posts and stories – there's a culture growing around the topic of ambition that praises it as something to be celebrated. And this is great – there's nothing wrong with ambition, of course. We should all feel empowered to use our energy in pursuit of the things we want the most.

What we're talking about in this section is not minimizing ambition, but harnessing it in the most effective way. There are a couple of problems that people frequently face in relation to the topic of ambition:

1. You're not ambitious enough

Sometimes, when we think about the topic of purpose, we get stuck. This might be because of the way we were educated or brought up, or it might be because of our current environment. The first step on the path to finding your purpose is to believe that it's possible to live a purpose-driven life – and not only is it possible, but it's actually highly likely that you'll be able to do it. You don't have to settle for anything less, despite what you might think or believe, or what other people might tell you. The path to living a purposeful life, full of depth and meaning, is just waiting for you to start pursuing it.

2. You get over-ambitious

On the other hand, some of us have extremely high ambitions. Again, this might come from the way we were educated or brought up, or it might just be an in-built sense of capability. And this is a good thing! But the danger of being overly ambitious is that you burn out fast, or become disappointed when things turn against you (sound familiar?). If you set your ambitions high, you also need to cultivate qualities of humility, empathy and self-compassion. As much as you want to experience the highs and lows of life, you want to also have a solid foundation to return to when things get difficult.

In some spiritual traditions, this is referred to as the 'ground of your being'. It's a place of deep, anchored stability where you find your true self – the self that isn't dependent on outward achievement or external wins. This is the most powerful tool when it comes to taming your ambition: the knowledge that you always come back to yourself, whether you're successful or unsuccessful in any particular goals you set. This is also a protection mechanism, because you start to learn that – regardless of external things that happen to you – you'll be okay if you keep returning to this foundation.

3. You move from one extreme to another

Some of us fall within this particular category: a mix of the under-ambitious and over-ambitious. Perhaps in some areas of our lives, we cultivate high ideals – maybe with our career, or in our physical health and wellness goals. And in other areas, perhaps we compromise – we might not feel like we deserve our relationship ideals, for example. Speaking from personal experience, it's possible to be both over-ambitious and under-ambitious about the same thing, sometimes in the same day. In fact, even a single piece of feedback or a comment from someone else (or simply our own change of perspective) can lead us in a different direction.

Human beings are complicated, and it's not particularly surprising that some of us are a little inconsistent when it comes to ambition – it's a difficult, multi-layered topic. One approach is to re-evaluate where your energy is currently going, and (if you feel like it's appropriate) re-orientate it towards goals that are receiving less of your energy and attention. Taking the example above, this might mean slowing down your career ambitions to dedicate a little extra time to personal relationships. Recalibrating your life in this way doesn't have to be dramatic – it can mean simply and slowly redirecting your focus towards new priorities.

The search for meaning

Let's return to Viktor Frankl. You'll probably have heard, at some point, of *Man's Search for Meaning* – Frankl's leading text in the field of logotherapy (a discipline sometimes summarized as 'a meaning-centered form of therapy or counselling'). Frankl believed that every human being contains 'spirit' – this wasn't necessarily a religious concept, but more of a universal human element. Within this spirit lies the movement towards meaning. Frankl believed humans have a will to discover this meaning, and that this will could fuel us to endure any suffering to pursue it. So, we are meaning-searching creatures, and the world is open to our interpretation.

One of the consequences of this way of looking at 'meaning' is that we no longer think about 'happiness', in the sense of being fully content in the present moment. An inner sense of happiness will often be a side-effect of the purpose-driven life, but we're going one layer deeper than that. We're focusing on growth: reaching from the place where we presently stand, towards a future version of ourselves, our lives and our existence. We are working with the fuel of potential. This might mean, at times, putting aside the pursuit of pleasure. Purpose-finding work isn't always comfortable, and there may be some aspects of it that are difficult. It's challenging to get to know yourself on an existential level, and many people choose not to go deeper. But the rewards of the work can be immeasurable, long-lasting and transformational.

To take another example, let's look at purpose-finding within spiritual traditions (big topic, but we'll attempt a brief example). Seeking meaning and purpose has always been an element of the religious journey. During my own monastic training, this was one of the key principles throughout the time we spent in our community. The idea of 'sacrificing' the self in service of 'something greater' – a greater sense of purpose – was one of the fundamental principles on which the entire programme turned.

Taking a broader view still, think about the 'non-religious spirituality' that has become a dominant theme in millennial culture. I imagine we can all think of that one person (it might be you) that feels spiritually connected doing certain things, like meditation, journaling, walking in nature or some kind of physical activity. In amongst that general feeling of 'spiritual connection', I'd guess there was also a feeling of ultimate purpose: a feeling of belonging in the world, like you have something to offer, or like you're here to give something back. You probably know from your own experience that life feels more full, more exciting, more vibrant, when you feel like you're 'connected' to something greater than yourself (whether that's other people or the world in general). There's 'spirituality' involved whenever you choose to go deeper, or reach beyond yourself. There might be an element of spirituality in cooking for a friend, or reading about quantum physics, or caring for your house plant. Whenever you get into a place of connection, of deeper meaning and purpose, there's often a sense of something 'bigger' going on.

I'm not sure that any particular route – religion, or logotherapy, or general spirituality – is the 'right' route. I think the choice is open to you: pursue the path that feels most aligned with what you believe about yourself and the world. Maybe even craft your own new path, if that feels like the most solid, stable ground on which to build your life. This book doesn't force you in a specific direction, but it does provide a starting point to the work. For thousands of years, human beings have been meaning-seeking animals, and that doesn't seem likely to change any time soon. One of the most important skills we can practise, then, is the ability to explore purpose in our lives.

A note on privilege

Purpose-finding work, existential analysis and logotherapy is, in some respects, a privilege to undertake. Most people don't get an opportunity to really analyse and structure their lives in the very deliberate, careful, thoughtful way that you – as a reader of this book – are adopting. Sometimes this is because of the cultural or social context; in other cases it's because of a lack of time or resources or awareness. Sometimes it's even the case that having a comfortable, settled lifestyle can mean that this work isn't necessary. A lot of people move through life without feeling the call to find their purpose.

I'm assuming, if you've picked up this book and read this far, that you probably don't fall into any of the categories above. You're probably someone (like me) who is a little existentially restless, or someone who is searching for direction. Before you read on, then, just take a moment to appreciate that this is actually a position of privilege. It's a gift to be able to look at your life in detail, and make changes where you can. It's a gift to be struggling with these questions, even if they feel difficult and exhausting and confusing. It's a gift that not everyone gets to experience. There are two important points here: appreciation, and giving back.

The first – appreciation – is straightforward. As you progress through this book, see if you can approach the work from a position of gratitude. To even get to be doing this work means that you're alive, you're fully awake, you're ready to shape and form and *participate* in your life. You're *living*, not just existing.

The second – giving back – is a longer-term project. This means that, whenever you get the opportunity to talk to other people about their purpose, or whenever you mentor or supervise or instruct people with less experience than you, you start to give this work back. This can be in the subtlest of ways – you can talk about your own purpose-finding journey, or you can recommend books (maybe even this one!), podcasts or other resources. Remember that – just like you – people will come to their own purpose-finding journey when they're ready, so don't force it on anyone. But sharing your progress (and your failures and struggles, as well as your successes) can be inspiration for others to begin.

If you're looking for specific organizations to get involved with, or various ways you might be able to give this work back to the world, check out the 'Resources' chapter.

The challenges of everyday life

Life is hard. It's hard in ways we imagined (responsibilities, finances, relationships) and ways we never expected (pandemics, career changes, existential crises). Even with the best of intentions, it's easy to lose sight of any sense of ultimate purpose amongst our day-to-day challenges and struggles. Our lives in the modern world are fast, and our goal is often to speed them up – as if we're trying to get somewhere. Often, we haven't ever considered exactly where it is we're trying to get to. Or, more fundamentally, *why* it is we're trying to get there in the first place.

The thing is, we're one of the first generations to really ever have this problem. Our parents and grand-parents might have focused on work, family and other cultural demands, and the generation before that would have endured huge social shifts during wartime. If, like me, you were born in a democratic country, with relatively stable personal circumstances, we have the immense gift of being able to shape and form our lives in a variety of ways. But with this gift comes pres-sure – the pressure to 'get it right', to avoid regrets, to make the most of our freedom and our opportu-nities. And so, even though we're part of a culture of abundance, we're stressed, worried and anxious about it. We can't sleep properly, or we're burned out, or we're too exhausted to try any more. We've lost sight of what we want to be doing amongst all the possibil-ities of what we *could* be doing.

One thing I noticed during my time training in a monastic community was that it was much easier to keep sight of the overall goal. This was because the architecture of our everyday life was specifically orientated towards the purpose of the programme (which was to devote a year of our lives to the community). Our time was ordered according to a structure of rituals, habits and practices, which all pointed us back towards the overarching 'mission'. It wasn't possible to lose sight of where we were headed, because we were consistently checking back in. Even during the most hectic part of my working week, I knew I'd be coming back to the community space, part of a larger programme with a larger goal in mind. It's something that's often seen in community settings – not just religious communities, but any group with a consistent theme and unified narrative. There's usually something that makes the whole thing fit together: a sense of enduring mission, or an agreed direction that each group member is able to hold in their mind. Something that reassures people that they belong, that they're part of something bigger and that they're on the right path.

Think about some examples from our society today. Politics might be an obvious illustration of the power of a dominant narrative. Unfortunately, it also shows the power of a narrative to fragment and divide people – but it's possible for people to be united under the same mechanisms. Or, think of any experience where you've felt connected to other people – a live music event, for example, or a comedy show where you're laughing alongside others. For sure, this phenomenon is something that shows up in religion, but it doesn't belong exclusively to it. And it's unlikely that religion 'created' this community power – it most likely just harnesses impulses (for solidarity, connection and common goals) that were already inherent within us.

There are a few lessons in here that could be helpful for the purpose-finding path. Some of them (community, mission, goal-setting) we'll come on to later. But one of them we'll cover now: the significance of practice.

The significance of practice

When I trained in a monastic setting, our retreat days had a rhythm to them. Wake up, morning prayer. Breakfast, in silence. Reading, study, tasks around the house and in the garden. Cups of tea. More silence, more tasks around the house, cooking, eating, study. Evening prayer. Sleep.

I was never religious growing up, so this was all new to me. But it felt *so* natural, like I was supposed to have been living this way all along. It was almost as if my life was finding a rhythm that it had always been designed for, but that I had covered up with endless emails and weekends in the office and constant phone notifications. As the year in training progressed, I learned more and more about the importance of practice when it comes to the spiritual life. I learned that practice is, in fact, a matter of retraining the patterns of your life to reflect the person you want to be, and the type of life you want to live. I learned that practising things like prayer and reflection actually encouraged my own brain to be more reflective, more contemplative, more settled.

In the modern world, we want a quick fix for things. The constant churn of capitalist culture has taught us that quicker, faster and cheaper is better. We're taught that having more of the next newest thing is always the goal, and that we won't ever be satisfied unless we stay in constant pursuit of it. If something seems difficult, or out of reach, or requires a significant amount of dedicated practice, we're often not interested. The rewards are too intangible; the promise of achievement is too far off. In many cases, we've forgotten the value of deliberate, intentional work, designed to achieve a long-term result.

Let's think about practice in a different context. Imagine your favourite sportsperson, or your favourite actor. In fact, imagine *anyone* who has cultivated a particular skill over a long period of time. In each and every case, there was a consistent element: practice. It's true that people are naturally gifted – musical geniuses, or athletes physically built in a certain way that suits a certain sport, and so on. But for each and every wildly successful person, in their given field, there will be an element of consistent, repeated practice.

One more example of practice, from my own life. I was born into a family of musicians, and grew up performing a variety of instruments. I was in choirs, orchestras and chamber groups; I performed solo and in ensembles and in front of examiners. And the defining thing I remember about these years was the *practice*. I remember the performances too, of course – the few moments of success or achievement – but what I really remember was the hard, slow process of practice. Hours and hours of practice, every single day, for months. I'm telling you about this because it shows the reality of working towards, well, pretty much anything. Practice lies behind every trophy, every glossy achievement, every overnight success (or at least, the ones that reward skill). It's often messy and difficult and frustrating, and yet, it's the key to moving *forwards,* both personally and in the world.

Just like everything else, purpose-focused work is a practice. It's not a one-off event, or something you can tick off your list after an afternoon's work. Instead, purpose-focused work is something you carry with you, for the rest of your life. Because – and this is a positive thing, I think – for as long as you keep growing and evolving and developing, your purpose will expand along with you.

The downside of practice is that, well – it seems like a lot of work. Even the word 'practice' sounds uninteresting. But purpose-finding practice doesn't have to feel like work (even if it is, in a broader sense, the 'work' of figuring out your life). As you approach the exercises in this book, I'd encourage you to treat them as an artistic or creative project – something to be carefully considered and treated with integrity; something to be worked on slowly, with intention. And you can't fail at this work. There are no right or wrong answers – just a steady process of discovering yourself.

We talk about 'lifestyle' a lot, in the generation of social media. In part, the concept of 'lifestyle' is appealing to us because it gives us a level of control – artistic design – over our lives. This is the perspective I'd encourage you to take when it comes to purpose-finding work. It might be challenging, but it's also empowering, and personal, and – hopefully, eventually – a work of art.

There's more on the practice of purpose in Chapter 5, but for now – let's get into some basic purpose-finding exercises.

CHAPTER 3

FINDING YOUR PATH

Eight purpose-finding exercises for your toolkit

This is where the real work starts. In this chapter, you'll be offered eight major purpose-focused exercises, ranging from mission statements to self-awareness challenges, from vision-building to story development, and much more.

These exercises are significant, and they take some time commitment (this is the work of figuring out your life, after all). But they're worth it. Feel free to work through this chapter in order, or select and revisit your favourite practices over time.

Mission statements

Writing time: 30 minutes

Preparation: a plain sheet of paper and a pen

Recommended practice: return to your statement once a month to review and revise

We're starting broad. You might remember that we tried out a short mission statement exercise in Chapter 1, but this time we're taking a deeper, slightly different approach. This mission statement is going to be your framework for the road ahead; a place to identify and articulate your most important vision. Here are a few key principles to bear in mind as you approach this exercise.

1. Keep it brief

We'll come into the detail of your personal mission, values and principles in later exercises. For now, keep it brief. Your mission statement should be – ideally – a single sentence. It's okay if you start off longer, but you should be looking to refine until you end up with the bare framework of your path. It's also okay if you start off shorter (maybe only a few words come to mind, at first), but aim to build it out a little. We'll come on to some examples later in this exercise.

2. Keep it high-level

As a template, consider a corporate mission statement. Corporate mission statements generally don't change dramatically over the course of the business's evolution. Take Amazon, for example – its origin (books) is very different to where it's ended up, but this mission statement could still apply:

> We aim to be Earth's most customer centric company. Our mission is to continually raise the bar of the customer experience by using the internet and technology to help consumers find, discover and buy anything, and empower businesses and content creators to maximise their success.[6]

Of course, a corporate mission statement is a little easier to map out than a personal mission statement (we can often make a business plan with much more ease and predictability than we can plan for our own lives) but the same concepts remain. Imagine your life five years from now. Could you apply the same mission statement? Would it work? And more importantly, would you still *want* it to? If you don't think your mission statement is sufficiently high-level to move and evolve with you over time, think about revising.

One final point: the mission statement doesn't have to apply specifically to every area of your life (it would be pretty impressive if that could be done in a single line!). Instead, think of it as your guiding charter – all of

---

[6] www.aboutamazon.co.uk/uk-investment/our-mission

the other complexities of life fit beneath it, but remain aligned with the general direction of the statement.

3. Make it unique

This part might take a little time to figure out. We're all unique beings, with individual passions and preferences and dreams. But it can be hard to translate that from your inner awareness to a set of words on the page. For that reason, it's a good idea to do this exercise alone, at least to begin with: sometimes reviewing or assisting with someone else's mission statement can have an influence on the development of our own.

If you still don't feel like your words are accurately reflecting the personal qualities and 'essence' of what you want to convey, try stepping away from the work for a while, and returning after you've had a chance to reflect.

With those major principles out of the way, let's get started.

First step

Make a list of all the things you've valued most from your past, all the things that are most important to you at present, and all the things you want in the world. These three areas (the things you've had, the things you have and the things you want) are a map of your desired past, your present and your future. This is your foundation for building your mission statement.

Second step

Go through your three lists (past, present, future) and figure out if there are any commonalities, or consistent themes. For example, the 'future' column might reflect a desire for a family, and the 'present' column might include close friendships. The common theme here might be community, or close personal relationships.

Using a career-focused example, the 'present' column might include your current working environment, and the 'past' column might include previous work experience you've had, but the 'future' column might reflect a different kind of desired career experience. The common theme here might be success, or ambition, or intellectual development.

If you can't find a common theme between your 'future', 'present' and 'past' lists, think about the elements that seem most important to you – which aspects stand out to you as key priorities?

Third step

Once you have the key elements narrowed down, it's time to craft your language. Mission statements often work best with powerful, assertive language – they

43

should be confident, goal-orientated and bold. To start, you can use the phrase: 'my mission is...' – and then you can remove this part once you have your statement.

Here's a basic example:

> My mission is... to be an inspiration to my community, and to lead a balanced life.

This mission statement identifies two aspects: community and self-care. One is externally focused (inspiring others), and the other is internally focused (making sure the author's life is set up in a balanced way). Notice, too, the things that are not present within this mission statement – career goals, or big ambitions about changing the world. That's not to say they won't have a place in *your* mission statement, but it does demonstrate what is important to this particular person.

Another example:

> My mission is... to use my natural abilities as a team leader to encourage positive change.

This mission statement draws on the author's personal talents, and works on the basis that the individual has enough self-awareness to recognize their own abilities (in this example, leadership). This self-awareness might have come through personal development work, or it might be a product of feedback, formal reviews or mentoring (you'll see, as you work through this chapter, that many of the exercises can inform and enhance other exercises). The second part of the statement focuses on the impact of the author's skills: a clear assertion that the author will be utilizing their skill-set to try and make a difference.

As with the first example, notice what isn't present in this mission statement – a focus on the self, or on close personal relationships. Again, this isn't about being correct or incorrect, but more about having a helpful exercise to draw out your own priorities. It's possible that you'll discover things about yourself that weren't clear to you before.

Final step

As with many of the exercises in this chapter, the mission statement will help you most if you go back to it regularly to refine and revise. Your priorities will change over the course of your life – probably more frequently than you're conscious of – and the mission statement exercise is a great way to stay connected to your path. Try revisiting the statement every month to check it still works for you, and to incorporate any changes you feel are relevant. You can also keep your mission statement somewhere visible (perhaps make it your phone lock-screen or your desktop background, or keep it pinned to your wall somewhere) so you can continue to check in with it.

(*A final note*: you should never feel defined or restricted by your mission statement. This exercise should serve *you*, not the other way around. If you look at your mission statement and think that it just doesn't reflect you any more, or you feel like you've moved on from that place, review and rewrite. It might even be an insightful exercise to track your own evolution over the years by gathering your past mission statements in one place and seeing how they change over time.)

Self-awareness exercises

Writing time: 15 minutes for each exercise

Preparation: a notepad or folder, and a pen

Recommended practice: pick an exercise to complete every week; return to the ones that are the most helpful for you

This section will take you through a couple of brief self-awareness exercises. Pick and choose your favourites, or work through them in a single notepad to figure out commonalities and consistent themes. Each exercise alone may not deliver huge insights or personal revelations, but taken together – and integrated with the other practices in this book – you'll start to develop a more comprehensive sense of self-awareness.

Exercise 1: the foundational 'why'[7]

In this exercise, you're going to start with a statement, beginning with the words: 'I want'. The statement can relate to anything you like: career, relationship, health, or other goals and ambitions. Here are a few examples:

I want a promotion in the next six months.

I want to earn [a certain amount of money] by the time I'm 35.

I want to find a partner and start a family.

I want to meet all my health and fitness goals by the end of the year.

Once you have your statement, you're going to start unravelling it by repeating the response: 'why?'. If it helps to lay it out in a visual way, you can start with the statement at the top of the page and work down with arrows (similar to a flow-chart). Here's a worked example:

I want a promotion in the next six months.

---

[7] Sometimes also known as the 'Five Why Method'. See: https://en.wikipedia.org/wiki/Five_whys

WHY?

To reach my career goals and develop my professional reputation.

WHY?

To feel more comfortable about my career path, and know that I'm on the right track.

WHY?

To have a general sense of life satisfaction, and feel proud of myself for my achievements.

At some point, you can stop the exercise – there'll probably be a natural point where your last 'why' taps into something deep and instinctive, or something that feels like a natural ending to the series of questions. This is sometimes known as your 'foundational why': the 'why' behind all the other 'whys'. But if you reach a final answer that doesn't feel right, you have a couple of options. You can either work back up the chain of 'why', and see if you want to offer a different response to any of the answers you gave. Or, you can reconsider your first statement as a whole (i.e. the statement that led to the chain of 'whys'), and see if it would be helpful to reassess it.

For example, taking the job promotion example above, if you felt like the final answer (life satisfaction) didn't line up with the initial statement (job promotion), you could use it as an opportunity to rethink. Is there anything else that could deliver life satisfaction in the same way? Is a job promotion really likely to lead to the outcome you want? There are no right or wrong outcomes: the point is just to get to the heart of your life choices.

_____

Exercise 2: the rule of life

This is a practice I learned during my time in a monastic community, and it's something that became central to my experience of the year. It's a practice we referred to as 'the rule of life' (the name sounds more dramatic than it is, I promise). The 'rule of life' was essentially a statement of values and principles that we, as members of a community, agreed to shape our lives around. The 'rule of life' title might actually be a little misleading, since it wasn't a strict 'rule' (in the sense that breaking it would have negative consequences). Instead, it was more of an aspirational collection of overarching values that we agreed, as a community, to structure our lives upon.

Here are some (generalized!) examples from our rule of life:

- *Silence*: we agreed to make space for silence within our year in the community, and take time to reflect and be in the present moment. During times of retreat, periods of silence were

structured into our day. In our non-retreat
lives, we were encouraged to carve out periods
of silence for ourselves.

- *Study and self-development*: we agreed to make
study and learning (about ourselves, as well as
about theology and philosophy) a central part
of our experience.
- *Service with compassion*: we set ourselves the
objective to serve each other and people we
encountered in the world with compassion,
grace and generosity.

So – you get the idea. These are high-level principles and values that can be applied in a lot of different ways, in a lot of different contexts, over a long
period of time. They can also be interpreted differently, depending on the individual applying them. In
this exercise, we'll work through how to create your
own rule of life.

Take a sheet of paper and start by brainstorm-
ing your key personal values and principles. In
Appendix 1, you'll find a list of suggestions for
personal values, so feel free to find inspiration there
– but make sure anything you select feels personal
to you. Once you have your collection of values (no
limit on how many you can add, but make sure to
prioritize your most important ones), you can start
to craft your own rule of life.

Begin by taking a single principle: let's say, for example, *generosity*. Maybe this is one of your key values. Write the word 'generosity' as your heading, and write a short paragraph underneath (3–4 lines works best) about the importance of this characteristic and how you intend to uphold it. Here's a worked example.

Generosity

> Generosity involves giving away my privileges and gifts so that other people can benefit. I practise generosity because I understand my connection to others, and I want to use my talents, abilities and opportunities to help, where I can. I intend to take every chance to be generous, and I will continually look for ways in which I can give back to others.

Once you've completed one principle, repeat with the others. You're aiming for between seven and ten: not too many that it becomes vague and generalized, but not too few that it becomes overly focused on a singular aspect. Remember, it's *your* rule of life – make sure you're being honest about the things that matter most to you. Not every principle has to be focused on other people: you can include things like wellbeing, self-care and self-improvement. As with all of the exercises in this book, you're welcome to return to your rule of life at any time and amend or adjust as you feel appropriate.

Exercise 3: one-sentence feedback challenge

This one can feel a little awkward, so bear with me. This is also the first point at which you start to expand your purpose-finding work beyond you and your notebook, so it can be a bit of a hurdle (feel free to mark this exercise to return to at a later date, if you prefer).

In this exercise, you're going to start gathering feedback from other people about what *they* think your purpose is. This is not intended to shape you into the intentions or desires of other people, but just to enable you to formulate a well-rounded view of how you come across in the world. Sometimes, our own perceptions of our lives become so entrenched (and so deeply personal) that it can become difficult to see beyond them. This exercise helps you to take a broader view.

The exercise is similar to 'upward mentoring', which is becoming more and more common in professional organizations. The goal is to obtain feedback you wouldn't normally get, so that you can start to understand the external perception of yourself with a little more clarity. In the context of a professional organization, this might mean a boss or senior leader seeking feedback from people 'lower down' the career hierarchy.

For you, it just means seeking out feedback from people that you wouldn't normally receive it from.

First, gather 3–5 people that you trust. Try to avoid the people you're closest to (partner, close family member), and go for people who know you well, but not *too* well. You're looking for a (relatively) objective perspective.

Once you have your 3–5 people, choose a method of communication that's appropriate: not too formal (email might be a bit much), and not too direct (probably don't ask on the phone or on a video call). Text is great, or other messaging platform – something private, but relaxed. Then, choose a way to frame your question.

The intent of this exercise is to obtain feedback, but the specific choice of language is your own. You can choose whether to ask about a certain aspect of your character, or a particular personality trait, or just ask a general open-ended question. Here are a couple of examples:

- What was your first impression of me?
- How would you describe me in a single sentence?
- What kind of person do you think I am, if you had to summarize?
- What are my best and worst qualities?
- What do you think I could improve on, as a person?

53

Don't feel limited to using one of the examples above, either – choose a question that feels like it will get you the most useful response. Keep it short and simple – and let them know it's just for your personal use. A couple of further tips, as you prepare for this exercise:

1. Give the person a bit of background – tell them you're doing a personal development exercise, and you're interested in their thoughts. Mention that you want them to be honest and that they don't have to prepare anything.

2. If they ask for time to think about it, or if they don't want to get involved for any reason, don't push it. This doesn't have to be a formal exercise, and you can always ask someone else.

3. When you do get feedback, it will probably be positive (it's unlikely that anyone close to you will say something explicitly negative to you directly!), but see if you can draw out the main themes or consistent points that are being expressed. This is much easier to do when you have an accumulation of feedback from 3–5 people: it becomes easier to pick out overarching ideas.

4. Bear in mind that the feedback will probably be focused on general behaviours, rather than specific habits. For example, people are much more likely to end up discussing character

traits, or what 'type' of person they see you as, rather than specific qualities they like or dislike. This is still insightful, so make sure you capture it in some way – you could take a couple of notes in a journal, or integrate it into your existing personal development notes.

5. Final thing: whatever you learn about yourself, try not to be offended. Remember that you don't have to accept all feedback as *objectively true* in order for it to be *helpful*. Even if you don't agree with an opinion, it still teaches you something about yourself and about your relationship with the other person. This process is all part of knowing yourself (including your friendships, relationships and interactions with others) better.

Vision-building

Writing time: 30 minutes for each session

Preparation: a notebook, sketchbook or journal

Recommended practice: return to the practice once a month (or when significant life events occur) to rework and revise your story

Time to craft your story. You'll have probably heard it said before, but it's true: human beings live according to stories. Whatever you believe about yourself, or about the world, probably comes from some kind of story you've been told. Whether you're spiritual or an atheist, whether you're conservative or liberal, whether you're vegan or not – these are all frequently debated topics, but at the heart of each of them is a story. That doesn't necessarily mean the story is made up: many of the stories we tell in our society are supported by evidence and backed up by data. But we *remember* and *retain* information best when it's presented to us in the form of a story, and over time this story can become our own story; our beliefs, values and principles.

All that is to say: it's important to get the story right. Most people never even think about crafting their own story, but it can be fundamental to designing the life you want. So, this section is an introduction to self-focused storytelling. Who do you want to be? You *always* get to choose.

First step

We'll start at the beginning. The first step is about mapping out your past – from the moment you were born to the moment you're reading this, right now. Mapping out your past is, of course, an immensely complex exercise, and you shouldn't expect it to be straightforward or something you can do in one sitting.

However, I'd encourage you to keep this exercise light. When we reflect on our past, there are likely to be difficult things, as well as the more positive experiences we've had. When difficult experiences do surface, it might be best to talk them through with someone – a therapist, or a close friend or family member. This exercise shouldn't *replace* that process: this is more about mapping out, in general terms, where your life has led you so far.

With that said, here are a couple of methods you can use to map out the past.

1. *Defining eras.* This method involves looking back over your life so far and picking out the key eras that defined your time. A good time period to map out as an individual era might be 5–7 years (perhaps with a slightly longer period for your childhood years). So, your eras might look something like this:

   0–10: childhood
   10–16: early teenage years
   16–20: late teenage years
   20–28: early adulthood
   28–40: adulthood
   (and so on – you can design the eras that make the most sense to you.)

   The idea is just to get a general sense of the phases your life has moved through. You don't have to be too specific with dates and years, since you're just aiming for an overall 'shape' in your mind, rather than a particular timeline.

2. *Defining phases.* This method reflects the specific external affiliations you've had during your life. So, for example, you could map something like this:

0–16: school
16–21: sixth form/higher education
21–28: first job
28–35: second job
(and so on – obviously specific to you.)

One benefit of this method is that it's clearer to map, since you'll know the dates of the relevant phases already. And it's also likely to fit naturally with your sense of how your life has developed, since these kinds of external affiliations are often the things that shape our sense of time over the years.

3. *Defining relationships.* This method works well if you've had key relationships at every stage of life, which have coloured your perception of your own experience. Not everyone will find this useful, since many of us will have had key defining periods without dominant relationships at play. But, if you're someone who has (for example) always lived with others, or always been in a partnership with someone

else, these relationships might be a key aspect of mapping out your past.

For example:

0–16: childhood home/family
16–21: friends/university house
21–28: partner 1
28–35: partner 2/marriage
35: marriage/family
(and so on – this is just a generalized example.)

The benefit of working with this structure is that it brings other people into consideration. If you've always been someone whose life is inextricably connected with others, it might be helpful to integrate them into your map of the past. If, on the other hand, you're some-one who has spent long periods of time being independent, you might want to choose one of the other options (or define your own method for mapping things out!).

Second step

Your second step is going to take you to the future. This is where you record your five-year plan: a sense of what you want your life to look like in five years' time. This doesn't have to be detailed or specific. Try thinking about high-level aspects of life, like what you want to be doing with your time, or big things you want to have achieved. If you don't have specific goals for the future, you can add more intangible things – for example, the person you want to be in five years, or the qualities you want to develop, or any specific skill-set or abilities you want to gain.

For example:

> In five years' time, I want my life to encompass the following:
>
> 1. a property that I own;
> 2. a job in my industry that fulfils me and that offers me a route to career progression; and
> 3. a creative project (for example, a book) that is long-lasting and that I have worked on over a period of time.

If you'd like to replicate the 'era' approach from step one, you can divide up the next five years into a couple of small 'eras' – maybe corresponding to the goals you've set yourself (for example, the first 'era' of time to focus on the first goal, and so on). But again – no pressure, this is just to get a general sense of the direction in which you want things to head.

(*A quick note on planning for the future* – and this applies to any goal-setting exercise that you carry out. Things change over time, and life will probably take you in an unexpected direction. This can be a good thing! In some ways, the most **unexciting** outcome would be for all of your plans to perfectly execute themselves without any challenges or hurdles to overcome. Instead, you can see challenges as opportunities to make you stronger; more resilient; more motivated. Our plans aren't ruined by a change in direction, it just becomes another opportunity to practise agility of thought and creative, strategic responses. So, don't worry if things don't go the way you planned. You *always* get to choose how to respond, and you *always* have an opportunity to redesign your life according to your new circumstances.)

Third step

This step brings us right back to the present. You're going to lay out your past planning (step 1) and your future planning (step 2) in one place. And then you're going to take account of where you are right now.

For this 'present moment' exercise, you're going to record your thoughts to the following questions (brief bullet-points are fine):

1. How do I feel about the journey so far? What are the main thoughts or reflections that I have on my life up to now?
2. What kind of person am I becoming? What have my past experiences and encounters led me to believe about myself and the world?
3. What kind of person do I want to become in the future? Are there any lessons from my past

that I want to take forwards, to apply to my future goals and ambitions?

The intention of this exercise is to encourage you to see your life as a story, with you as the main character. The three questions above don't have fixed answers; you can't get them wrong (or right). Instead, you get to choose the qualities that take priority in your life; the kind of person you want to become; the way you feel about events that have happened to you so far. You're always in control of the narrative – and if you don't like the outcome of the exercise, start from step 1 and rewrite it.

Of course, there will be objective experiences, events and relationships that happened, and that were an important part of your past. But you *always* get to define how to integrate those experiences into your personal view of life. You can structure around them, make them part of your path, choose to learn lessons from them – whatever makes most sense for you. The important point is that you get to decide; you become the author of your own existential experience.

Annual review

Writing time: 45 minutes

Preparation: a journal or folder to hold your notes in, or keep a record digitally

Recommended practice: make your review once a year, at the same time each year. Check in with your review (including goals, progress and ambitions) and update every six months – or more frequently if you feel it would be helpful

I know this sounds like something your boss would impose on you, but it gets more interesting than that (I promise). An annual review is an opportunity to check in with yourself on a more substantive level than some of the other exercises. It gives you a chance to pause your life, take a good look at your surroundings, and decide whether you want to continue in the same direction, or whether things need to change. The practice of completing a yearly review, if performed consistently over time, also acts as a kind of personal 'autobiography': you're collecting moments of your life that, over time, form a bigger picture. It can actually be a tool for reflection and personal memory gathering, as well as strategic planning.

Here are the basic instructions for planning your first annual review.

First step

Decide when the review is going to begin. It doesn't have to be 1 January every year, but keeping a memorable date will help you to anchor the practice, and makes it more likely to be consistent over time. Other 'marker' dates could include: your birthday, 1 September (the start of a new academic year, in most cases), 31 December, or the beginning/end of any season. If you have a particular spiritual, religious or cultural tradition, you might find it helpful to use a date that has significance in that context.

Second step

Figure out how you'll record your information. For an old-school option, it can be helpful to have a dedicated journal or notebook for each year's annual review. This has the benefit of making it feel substantive and enduring – but if you prefer to do it digitally, that works too. The digital annual review has the benefit of being easily referenced throughout the year, and editable (in case you want to make amendments or updates). You can keep all of your yearly reviews in a single document, although make sure to back it up.

Third step

The annual review is shaped around three main categories.

First, what happened this year?

Second, what have you learned?

Third, what do you want to carry forwards into next year?

We'll cover each category in a little more detail, although you can feel free to add or amend as you see fit.

What happened this year?

This question covers the objective output of the year. Under this category, you can record – in bullet points, continuous paragraphs, diagrams, images or any other format you like – what happened. This includes:

- things you achieved;
- successes and failures;
- unexpected events;
- external barriers and challenges;
- health (physical and mental);
- finances (investments, outgoings, etc.);
- relationships (family, friends, partners);
- travel and notable memories;
- things you regret;
- things you're proud of;
- things that started or ended; and
- anything else you want to talk about that was relevant for you in the course of the year.

This exercise is best done without judgement, criticism or analysis: it's purely a recording exercise to get everything down. It might take you a while to remember the information, so you can always pause the exercise and return to it over time. Other ways to remember your year include:

- looking back over your phone photos or screenshots;
- scrolling back through social media accounts;
- looking back through your diary or calendar;
- checking previous journal entries or notes; or
- checking in with friends, family and colleagues to see what they remember about the year.

What have you learned?

After recording all of the relevant information, you're going to track back through and see what you learned from it. As you do this, the intention is to maintain a neutral perspective. This means you're aiming to assess the information from an objective standpoint (or, at least, as objective as you can get).

Neutrality is important, because our personal attachment to things that happened can hold us back from actually learning. This risk applies when things didn't go our way, or when we felt like we failed, or when we wish we'd done something differently. It *also* applies when we feel like things went really well, when we felt successful and when we thought we couldn't have improved on our performance. Both of these personal perspectives – failure and success – can be a barrier when it comes to the annual review process, because we're trying to review *information*, rather than feelings or emotions. In particular, we're trying to get information that could actually teach us something useful.

Consider the corporate context, as a template. When a company writes an annual review, they're presenting facts, data and statistics to their investors and stakeholders. Although there might be a cover sheet with a note from the chairman to say how they feel about the performance of the company during the year, the most important information is generally presented objectively. The intention is for an outside observer to receive an overview of the company's performance, and obtain objective measurements with which to compare against previous annual performances, or against other companies.

Obviously, we're not writing a corporate annual report – and we don't have all the objective data available that a company might have. But the general principle is similar. When you're looking to extract lessons from things that happened, see if you can take a step back. When you encounter a success, reverse-engineer it to see what it was that led to the success. When you encounter a failure, ask yourself what you can learn from it. Failure is often the biggest learning opportunity we're given, because it showed us, with certainty, what *didn't* work. And then, we have an opportunity to try again, and see what might work next time.

Here are a few questions to shape your annual report review:

- What could I have done differently?
- If I could give my former self a single message one year ago, what would I say?
- If I could give my future self a single message one year from today, what would I say?
- Did this year show me that I need to develop a different or enhanced set of skills? In what respect? How can I go about developing them in the future?
- Looking at my greatest success, what were the factors that led to it? Can I distil them into general principles to carry forwards with me?
- Looking at my biggest failure, what would I do differently? Were there any crucial missteps or errors that I know not to repeat next time?
- What characteristics have I developed this year? Who am I becoming? Is there anything I want to change about myself going forwards?
- Where have my energies been devoted this year? In general, is there anything I would change about the allocation of my time and effort for next year?
- Is there anything I've neglected this year? Anything I want to spend more time on next year? Anything I've put too much time into this year?

These are, of course, just suggestions – you'll develop your own sense of the best questions as you work through the process over time. When you do find an effective question, note it down – it helps to ask consistent questions over the years, so you can compare your answers in a more reliable way.

(*A side note*: this process may take some time, and you might find it helpful to space out your annual review work over the course of a week or so. Giving yourself time to pause and reflect between different stages of the work can help you retain a sense of clarity when it comes to reviewing your year.)

What do you want to carry forwards into next year?

Once you've worked through the section above, the final step is to transform your information into actionable steps.

For example, if the lessons you picked out were:

- a fear of failure held you back from achieving your goals;
- a lack of information prevented you from making effective decisions; and
- strong personal relationships meant you felt settled and grounded throughout the year,

then you could transform them into the following action points:

- work on your self-confidence by challenging yourself to take small steps outside your comfort zone;
- work on your education by dedicating time to information-gathering and studying; and
- maintain and nourish the strong relationships in your life.

The next step is to take these goals to an even more granular level, making them into practical, achievable steps and allocating them to a specific time period.

For example:

- Work on your self-confidence by challenging yourself to take small steps outside your comfort zone:
  - Set yourself one challenge every month – something that makes you feel a little uncomfortable, but that leads you to greater personal growth.
  - Start by planning out your challenges for the next three months:
    - Month 1:
    - Month 2:
    - Month 3:

- Work on your education by dedicating time to information-gathering and studying:
  - Decide how much time, realistically, you have in your life to allocate to this task.

Apportion your available time according to how important you think this goal is.

o Once you've decided the basic allocation of time, choose (at what time of the day, and which day of the week) a consistent study period to work on your self-education.

o Set yourself some knowledge-related goals (for example: *I want to master [a certain topic] by [a certain date]*), as well as some measurable targets or metrics by which to assess your progress.

• Maintain and nourish the strong relationships in your life:

o Work out what it was that helped you maintain those relationships during the previous year. Plan out time to continue to do those things.

o Consider any additional relationship-focused goals or objectives you could add in, perhaps also checking in with the other people in your life to get their reflections on the year.

(*A side note*: remember that even outstanding successes and achievements often require maintenance. It's sometimes the case that we achieve something and then rest on that achievement for a long period of time. This is fine – of course! – if it's what you want to do, but make sure it's an intentional choice. If

71

you're determined to keep moving forwards, you can use your successes to set yourself further goals for the future, building on your momentum.)

Final step

Make your annual report something worth keeping (remember that it also serves as a collection of memories from your year). You could get inspiration from one of the many corporate annual report examples online, or Google 'creative annual report templates'. If you're working on paper, make sure you store it somewhere memorable.

You can choose whether to share your annual report with others, or keep it as a private personal development project. If you have a mentor or coach, you might want to introduce the annual report into your sessions: it can help to have someone holding you accountable for your future goals and objectives.

After you complete your report, be clear with yourself about when you'll next check in. As above, a regular check-in every few months might be good, to keep you on track. At the very least, I'd recommend checking your report every six months. You might even find it helpful to craft a mini-version of the annual report (a half-yearly report) to provide an interim update.

Consultancy check

Writing time: 45 minutes

Preparation: a notepad and pen; all of your other personal development notes

Recommended practice: undertake an initial consultancy check and then return as frequently as feels helpful (try every three months)

Remaining with the corporate-inspired theme, this exercise is called the 'consultancy check'. Here, you'll take the position of an external consultant and begin to evaluate your own life.

You'll probably be aware of the role of a consultant (in this case, that's you), which is usually to work with a client (in this case, also you) to produce a set of recommendations about a particular business or project (in this case, your life). With the annual report exercise above, you looked at an overview of your year, covering all aspects within a general, holistic assessment. But with the consultancy check, you could choose to focus on – for example – your career, or your relationships, or your personal health and wellbeing.

You could also do an overall consultancy check without focusing on any specific aspect, of course. And another option might be to do a series of specialized checks and then review them all together. You get the idea: there are a lot of ways to personalize this exercise. Let's go through the basic steps.

First step

First up, let's define the role. Companies often bring in a consultant when they need an external, experienced, objective third party to provide an opinion on an aspect of their business. While you're not external to your own life, you are certainly the most experienced party when it comes to actually living it, and you can do your best to be objective. So, sounds like you're the right fit for the task. As you carry out the check, bear in mind:

- Your job is to look at information with an aim to: (1) find out what happened and why; and (2) make some plans or suggestions for the future. Like the annual report, this exercise has both a reflective and a forward-planning aspect to it.
- To get into the mindset of an external onlooker, you can start to question all the assumptions you make about your life, and the decisions that make up your everyday reality. What you can offer, from the external perspective, is a challenge to all the things that go unnoticed because they're habitual, or because they've never been any other way. Your task is to ask *why* things

have to be a certain way, and then suggest methods and strategies for improvement.

- Bear in mind that not every process in your life is fit for strategic optimization. The consultancy exercise is best applied to relatively unemotional aspects of life – think careers, finances or personal skill-sets. The exercise is less useful when applied to close relationships, emotional decisions or aspects of your life that are bound up with another person's interests. Consider picking a separate purpose-finding exercise from this chapter for those aspects – try one of the self-awareness exercises on pp. 46–55, for example.

Second step

This is where you produce your 'scope of work' (sometimes also referred to as a 'statement of work'). In this summary, you'll note down any aspects of your life you'll be assessing and the outcomes you're looking for. Most often, those outcomes will be general: you're looking for areas of improvement, things to work on or aspects to enhance. But, if you prefer, you can make your goals more specific. For example, you can run a consultancy check to figure out why a certain thing went wrong, or why you failed in one circumstance and succeeded in another.

Whatever you choose, make sure it's included in your scope of work: set out the scope of the project in the first line, and add a couple of lines with details about your objectives. Aim for 3–4 sentences as a maximum. For example:

Scope of work

The scope of work will take into account my career over the last 12 months. The intention will be to identify areas of improvement and suggest reasons that I haven't been able to obtain a promotion. The outcome will be a set of recommendations that I will seek to implement over the next 12 months.

Third step

Time to get to work! Sit down with your data (the evidence of how things went, even if this is just from memory) and get as much detail down as possible. As with the annual report, you might find it helps to take a few breaks (maybe plan out the initial exercise over a week or so) to get all the information down as objectively as you can.

Once you have your information down, take it to a physically different setting, or take a few days' break before you continue. Sounds a little dramatic, but you might find, psychologically, that some physical space (whether in terms of location or time) gives you a slightly different perspective.

When you're ready, start to craft your report. The report can be as long or as short as you like, and you can write it in any preferred format. Bear in mind that a traditional consultancy report will generally be as short as it can get without losing the key content or findings. It should also be clearly presented, with visuals (charts, images, graphics) where those might help comprehension.

A couple of features to consider as you put together your report:

1. *A summary page*. This is often used in corporate reports to highlight the key findings. Imagine you were presenting your report to the board of directors of a company, and you needed to present the clearest summary of your findings before they lost interest in your presentation. What would you want to say, most importantly, in 3–4 bullet points? What are your key findings? What are your key recommendations?

2. *Comparative analysis*. A frequent feature in consultancy reports is comparative analysis – an overview of the market and what competitors are doing. When it comes to making a personal consultancy check, you don't need to go into detail about what your peers and colleagues are

doing, but it might help to note down some achievements and actions of the people around you. This should generally be for inspiration purposes – if you can see someone doing something (or becoming someone) you admire, see if you can figure out *what* exactly it is that inspires you, and then work out if you can incorporate aspects of that – in your own, unique way – into your life and work.

3. *Market conditions.* A consultancy report will usually take into account the current conditions in the market. For a business that has had a particularly successful or unsuccessful year, this puts gains and losses into perspective. For you, it might explain why certain things happened the way they did (for example, moving house or changing careers). A page or two of your consultancy report focusing on the external, uncontrollable conditions of your life can be helpful in order to put everything else into perspective.

4. *Suggestions and recommendations.* In the final pages of the report, include your suggestions for improvement. These can be high-level and vague, and can correspond to elements of feedback you picked up during your review of the evidence.

When it comes to recommendations, try to be a little more specific – aim for about 5–10 recommendations to take forwards into your next chapter, and make them actionable. If you end up with a small number of 'big' recommendations, break them down into sub-points until you're left with practical, actionable steps.

5. *Assumptions*. The final piece of your report should include your assumptions, which will put your recommendations into context. Your assumptions will be things like: your health remaining good, your living conditions remaining stable, and so on – you can add the ones that apply to you. You don't have to include every assumption (seeing as we're all operating on assumptions when it comes to planning anything), but include the ones that seem most relevant. For example, if you're aiming to move cities or jobs, you might include that; if you're hoping to improve your physical fitness or health, you might include that. It's always interesting to come back to a previous consultancy check and see which assumptions played out as you expected (and which didn't). Even this becomes an opportunity to learn something.

Dream CV design

Writing time: 30–60 minutes

Preparation: CV template (either an existing preferred template, or one that you can find online)

Recommended practice: one initial practice to set up your dream CV, then repeat and refine as often as you find helpful (to correspond to your changing ambitions and goals)

Personally, I've never had much success with vision boards. As a stereotypical lawyer, I do much better with mapping out the future when my thoughts can be classified and organized in a consistent way, rather than working with images and concepts. If you are a visual learner, a traditional 'vision board' exercise might be great for you – there are lots of examples and templates online (and you can, of course, adjust this CV exercise to fit a more traditional vision board template). But this exercise is really for those who are sceptical of the whole 'vision board' project. This exercise enables you to explore your goals, desires and – yes – 'visions', without getting lost in the Pinterest aesthetic that normally dominates this practice.

First step

Locate and select your CV template. You probably already have a CV: one option is to strip out all the details from this, save it as a new version and fill it in according to the steps in this exercise. Alternatively, you might like to start afresh, perhaps with something more creative. There are a whole range of CV templates online – from artistic to strategic, and everything in-between. Choose something that works, and that feels 'editable' – you want to be able to revisit frequently and make updates over time.

Second step

On a blank sheet of paper, give yourself 30 minutes to write out your goals. Make them big – go for outrageous, inspirational, high-level goals. Things that you're not sure whether you'll ever achieve; things that you might never have said out loud. Be totally honest with yourself – put aside the voice in your head that says it's unrealistic. This is an exercise of ambition, of mapping out future desired experiences. Get it all down without judgement, analysis or critical thinking.

Third step

Start to reshape your goals into tangible, CV-appropriate experiences. This might take a little creative thinking, but there's usually a way to do it for every goal on your list. For example:

> Goal: have my articles published in major publications (i.e. ones that others have heard of and will recognize).

This goal is a little intangible (it doesn't state particular publications, or what kind of recognition), but it's still easy to work with. In the 'experience' or 'publications' section of your CV (or other appropriate section of your template), you could add:

> *Publications*:

> My work has been featured in major publications such as [*The New York Times*, *The Atlantic* and *The Wall Street Journal*]. I am frequently asked to present at conferences and deliver keynote speeches as a result of this work.

It doesn't need to be totally precise, and you can always leave the details (such as the names of publications) blank. The really valuable aspect of this work is the point at which you transfer your broad, intangible 'dreams' into CV-focused reality. The process of articulation will quickly make clear to you exactly what your dreams might look like, if they came to life. From there, you can work out whether you truly want them or not (this part might surprise you), and if you do, which tiny steps you might put into action to help you get there.

Returning to that last idea for a moment: you might figure out that, once your dreams are down on paper as a CV-related reality, you might no longer want them, or you might no longer want them in that form. For example, using the example above, you might realize that it's not actually writing and publishing an article that forms the basis of the goal, but the social recognition and reputation that comes along with it. Perhaps article-writing is not actually the ambition, but just the means to an end. Is it possible to *reframe* the end goal according to a passion that fits more authentically into your life? For example, could you reach the goal of 'public recognition' by another route, like starting a business, or a podcast, or doing more public speaking?

Feel free to leave parts of the CV blank or vague – for example, you might not bother filling out your job history, or you might replace this section with a variety of future roles you want to have. You can personalize categories like 'experience', 'awards', 'publications' (etc.) accordingly, and you might also find it helpful to design a CV summary or headline that fits the person you aspire to be.

Final step

The CV exercise is, at its heart, a vision-focused practice. As a result, it's helpful to display your work somewhere it can inspire you. Vision boards are traditionally displayed in a prominent wall-space (or, if you're digitally-native, as the background on your laptop or phone). You can do the same with your dream CV – try pinning it to your wall, or taking a photo that becomes your background. You should feel free to come back to the CV at any point and revise – it should, ultimately, reflect your *current* dreams, so if you feel it becomes outdated or you outgrow it, you can return and adjust.

Observation activities

Writing time: 5–10 minutes, throughout the course of a week

Preparation: a notepad and pen/the notes app on your phone

Recommended practice: commit to the activity for a week, review in a single session at the end of the week

This activity is less of a sit-down journaling exercise, and more of a 'lifestyle practice'. The intention is to bring a little more awareness to the realities of your daily life, to see what you notice about yourself and your path. The challenge is to undertake *one* observation activity in a single week, planning reminders during the week to keep yourself on track, and noting down your findings as you go. At the end of the week, you can schedule a review session with yourself, perhaps integrating your findings into a broader personal development plan or journal. Or, you might find that your observations give rise to questions you want to consider going forwards, or something that it would be helpful to discuss with your boss, or something you need to transfer to your to-do list.

Below is a list of suggested activities. As mentioned above, it's easiest to focus on one at a time, and a single week is normally a good period of time during which to track progress. But see what works best – you might like to combine certain activities to give you a more holistic perspective, or you could spread the activities out over a longer period of time (for example, a month).

Activity 1

During the course of the week, remind yourself of the following questions each day:

> When do I feel most alive?

> When do I feel most engaged?

> When do I feel most aligned with my life, or most connected to myself?

The aim here is to observe, not force – so the task is to simply *notice* what's happening in your life. You might find that you automatically remember to make a note when you encounter a feeling of 'aliveness', engagement or connection. Or, it might be that you track back through your memory every time you come to review the questions. Either approach should work, but there's no pressure to get an answer every time. You might not notice anything during the course of a week – if that's the case, you can always extend the exercise to take place over the course of a month. If you notice that you don't get answers to any of the questions over the course of the month, it might be a sign to rethink your current career or lifestyle, just in case there are changes you could make to bring yourself closer to a feeling of existential fulfilment.

Activity 2

During the course of the week, remind yourself of the following questions each day:

> When do I feel most challenged?
>
> When do I feel like I'm learning and growing the most?
>
> What am I doing when I reach a state of 'flow' (i.e. genuine engagement with an activity, to

the extent that you might lose track of time or context)?

As above, don't force the answers – just notice, and make notes when anything relevant arises. If you've already done Activity 1, you might find the same events are giving rise to the same answers – that can be a good sign, indicating that your life is integrated and that you're on a consistent path.

Activity 3

During the course of the week, remind yourself of the following questions each day:

> What am I doing when I feel most calm?
>
> What am I doing when I feel most 'myself'?
>
> What am I doing when I feel 'at home' in the world, and in my life?

For each of these answers, be as specific as you can. Note down the people you're with, the activity you're doing, any external factors that might be contributing to your perspective, and so on. The more detail the better – it's sometimes the case that tiny factors contribute to a greater shift in mood or emotion, and it's only once we unravel them step by step that we can begin to see the whole picture.

Activity review

At the end of your week (or longer, if you've extended the activity over a longer period of time), gather your notes in one place. You're going to pick out key themes, activities and events to be classified under the following headings:

Things that make me feel 'alive'

Things that make me feel engaged, aligned with myself or connected

Things that make me feel challenged

Things that make me feel like I'm learning, growing and developing

Things that take me into a state of flow

Things that make me feel calm

Things that make me feel like myself/'at home' in the world

I've used the word 'things' here as a general classification, but feel free to replace that with 'people', 'events', 'activities', and so on – anything that corresponds to the findings you had from your observations.

Once you have the findings, the next step is open to you. The observation activity will only take you to the place of *awareness*: the choice of how to react and respond to your findings is yours to determine.

Perhaps the findings will encourage you to focus on a new goal, or reorientate your career towards the things you're passionate about, or spend more time with the people who make you feel fully alive. Or, perhaps, the exercise shows you that the majority of your time is *already* spent doing the things that bring you the most fulfilment.

Either way, it's a worthwhile exercise to repeat every so often – perhaps whenever you feel like life gets a little hectic, or you lose sight of the bigger picture in the chaos of day-to-day existence. The biggest benefit of the practice is that it gives you a little space from your life – almost like the kind of space you can sometimes find in a meditation practice – and from that perspective of spaciousness, you can start to make new choices (or reinforce the existing choices that are serving you well!).

Your ikigai

Writing time: 45 minutes

Preparation: a notepad and pen

Recommended practice: an initial session to define and create your ikigai, then revisit over time to make sure it still aligns with your intentions

There are a lot of books out there covering the topic of ikigai, so I'll be brief with this one. 'Ikigai' is not a new concept, but it seems to have reached a new level of global popularity in the last few years. The term itself, *ikigai*, is a Japanese word that translates roughly as 'reason for being'. Your ikigai is essentially your purpose; your main motivation; your reason for getting up every day and continuing your work.[8]

It's a framework for organizing your thoughts about life – so it fits in well at the end of this chapter. You can use the findings and insights from the exercises above, and apply them to the ikigai exercise below (which starts to turn the focus *outwards*, and might give you some practical ideas for next steps). Here's how to begin working with the ikigai framework in your own life.

First step

Draw out your framework. This is traditionally made up of four overlapping circles:[9]

---

[8] According to Wikipedia: although the concept of ikigai has long been in Japanese culture, it was first popularized by Japanese psychiatrist and academic Mieko Kamiya in her 1966 book 生きがいについて (*ikigai ni tsuite, On the Meaning of Life*).

[9] The four circle diagram has been attributed to Mark Winn (2014), who in turn adopted the concept from Andrés Zuzunaga. At the time of writing, a full summary of sources can be found in this article: www.sloww.co/ikigai/

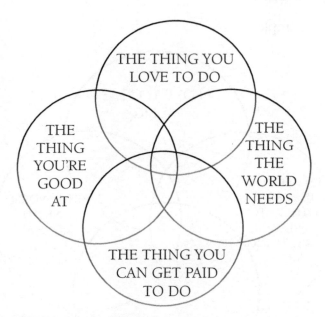

Top circle: the thing you love to do;
Right-hand circle: the thing the world needs;
Bottom circle: the thing you can get paid to do;
Left-hand circle: the thing you are good at.

The overlap of these circles (in the middle) is your ikigai.

Second step

Start to fill out the circles. In the example above, I've referred to a single 'thing', but if that thing isn't obvious to you, or if you feel like you want to include more than one thing, you can write down whatever comes to mind.

For example:

Top circle: playing a musical instrument;
Right-hand circle: art and creativity for inspiration;
Bottom circle: teaching music;
Left-hand circle: inspiring others to start music them-selves.

So, for this (fairly straightforward) example, your ikigai might be starting a music group, or teaching music to individuals.

It's important to note that your ikigai does not have to become your main path or career. Your ikigai might turn out to be a passion project you do at the weekends. Or, your ikigai might turn out to be family orientated: perhaps your ikigai is caring and looking after your own young children. In this case, your ikigai is integrated with the rest of your life – career, friendships, other passions – but doesn't necessarily need to be the *sole* thing you do with your time.

In short, the idea of an ikigai is flexible – you can play around with the concept, noting the overlaps and the corresponding or conflicting elements. You can (and probably should) revisit your ikigai over time – as your life evolves, so will your ikigai.

Third step

Put your findings into practice. As with all of the exercises in this book, the intention is to move from theory to practice, so that you can see the impact of redesigning your life according to your intentions. So, once you have your ikigai, mix and match it with one of the more practical exercises coming up in Chapter 4. For example, use your ikigai to shape your goal-setting as you approach Chapter 4's goal-setting techniques. Or, integrate your ikigai into Chapter 4's development plan. You could also try fitting your ikigai into the dream CV exercise outlined above, on pp. 80–84.

On a more basic level, you might want to display your ikigai somewhere as a reminder for yourself. You can do this by printing or refining your ikigai diagram and placing it somewhere visible (noticeboard, back of your wardrobe door, etc.). You could also make it the lock screen on your phone or the background on your laptop. Ideally, you want it somewhere you'll look at frequently, but not too prominent that it just becomes another unnoticed part of the environment. You could also set yourself reminders to return to your ikigai every few months, to ensure you're still aligned with your own design.

A QUICK NOTE ON WHERE WE'RE AT

The exercises in this chapter are designed to give you a starting point to approach the question of purpose. But they don't necessarily promise a perfect, simple answer. Their intention is, instead, to enable you to access the depths of your life – to explore your thoughts, feelings, ambitions, hopes, dreams, fears and everything in-between.

As you change over time, so will your responses to these exercises, so feel free to return and revisit as many times as you like.

In the next chapter, we'll explore a few more exercises, with a slightly more practical approach.

CHAPTER 4

DEVELOPING YOUR PATH

Five further exercises

In this chapter, we'll build on the work we began in Chapter 3. We'll start to look forwards, mapping out the future with goal-setting strategies, tracking tools and development plans.

Along with the exercises in Chapter 3, this section is the biggest part of the work. So, as above, feel free to take your time, work through this chapter in order or pick and choose as you like, and return whenever you're in need of new inspiration.

Goal-setting

Writing time: 30 minutes, repeat weekly

Preparation: a notepad and pen, or personal diary/calendar

Recommended practice: spend an initial session getting your goals down on paper, and return at a consistent time each week to check in on progress

There are a lot of ways to set goals. You've probably heard of a few of them already: 'SMART' goals, five-year plans, targeted goals, etc. In this section, I'll take you through the goal-setting practice that has been most effective for me over the years: macro, micro and daily goals. It sounds like a lot, but it's a method that gives you both something to aspire to, and something to achieve on a practical, day-to-day level. It's the *combination* of these aspects that makes it an effective system. Here's how to do it.

Macro goals

Let's start by defining your macro goals. The word 'macro' comes from a Greek word meaning 'large', so these are your biggest goals. You can choose the time period they apply to (for example, six-month goals or annual goals), but somewhere between three and 18 months is about right. Below that is a little too short-term for this method, and above that is hard to project with any specificity.

You're looking to gather around 3–5 of these macro goals – if you have more than that on your list, pick the ones you want to give most attention to. You know that aphorism, the art of attention is knowing what to say no to? Well, it's true for your goals. The fewer goals you have, the easier it will be to focus your full attention and energy on working towards them.

Here's a worked example, to start.

Goal 1: to improve physical fitness and overall health

Goal 2: to get a promotion at work

Goal 3: to build my online and social media presence/develop my personal brand

You can see from these goals that they're both *high-level* and *non-specific*: they could be achieved in a number of ways, and they are fairly open-ended. It might also be the case that your goals overlap in various ways (for example, Goal 3 on the list above could actually become a micro goal – see below – for Goal 2). If this is getting a little complex, don't worry: in the next step, we're breaking everything down.

Micro goals

Once you have your macro goals, it's time to get specific about how you want to achieve them. The word 'micro' comes from a Greek word meaning (you guessed it) 'small', so this is where you get a little more detailed. Using your macro goals from the step above, you're going to break them down. Each macro goal is going to give rise to around 3–5 micro goals.

Here's the worked example again, starting with the macro goal and breaking it down into the micro goals:

Goal 1: to improve physical fitness and overall health

1. start running every other day;
2. hold myself accountable for progress by tracking myself on an app;
3. search for a community of other people interested in running, so I can be part of a group with similar goals.

Goal 2: to get a promotion at work

1. research possible strategies for promotion; decide which position I want to aim for;
2. reverse-engineer the job description for that position so I can work out which skill-set is required for the role;

3. speak to people already in a similar role to obtain their advice and guidance on my progress.

Goal 3: to build my online and social media presence/develop my personal brand

1. review my entire online presence; decide which platforms to focus on;
2. decide what my personal brand actually is (perhaps take a course in personal branding, or research podcasts/books that might help);
3. set myself a consistent target for posting content online each week.

These are, of course, just examples – but you get the picture. Your micro goals should conform to the following guidelines:

1. they should be practical – obvious, straightforward actions;
2. they should be well-defined – make it clear what you want to achieve;
3. they should be specific – don't go for big, vague objectives;
4. they should be attainable – if it feels like an unmanageable goal, see if you can break it down even further; and
5. they should be linked to an action, rather than a theoretical or intangible outcome.

Daily goals

This is the final part of the goal-setting system, and it's a chance for you to integrate both macro and micro into the structure of your day-to-day life. For this step, you're going to be transferring your micro goals into your current planning system. The specific steps will depend on which system you currently use to structure your days. For example:

- If you work with a paper diary, you can schedule in deadlines for your micro goal achievement. If you work with a calendar, you can do the same, or try allocating tasks to each individual day.
- If you work with an app on your phone (for example, a calendar app or habits tracker), you can transfer your goals into it. Try setting daily habits that correspond to the goals you want to achieve, or use a self-imposed deadline to set a time limit on goal achievement.
- If you use a daily planner or to-do list, you can break down your goals until they reflect daily tasks, and then schedule them in accordingly. If you have a goal that needs to be broken into repeated daily tasks (i.e. a goal like writing or working on a specific project, which needs to be done every day), it might help to divide your goal into sections, and schedule a section each day. For example, if you're writing a 10,000-word

essay, you can break it into ten sets of 1,000 words and schedule a set for each day.

- If you prefer time-blocking approaches, you can work out how long each micro goal is going to take, and then block off the appropriate amount of time in your calendar (paper or app form). This is similar to the idea of scheduling meetings with yourself, and can be quite effective – as long as you stick to the schedule, or reorganize missed sessions if they occur.

- Other planning tools include the notes app on your phone (for a daily to-do list or checklist for outstanding things), reminders (either physical, written down and displayed somewhere, or digital) and countdowns. The latter can be particularly effective if your goal has a clear deadline, because it focuses your mind on the sense of urgency required.

To help you stay on track, frequently refer back to your macro and micro goals as you complete your daily goals. The three elements should always work together, so if you feel like your daily goals are taking you in a different direction, you can either:

1. reassess your macro goals – maybe you want to realign or readjust, based on the feedback or progress from your daily goals; or
2. recalibrate your micro goals to give you a different set of objectives. Sometimes we try

things to achieve a macro goal and it doesn't work out, or it's not effective, or we realize things could be done a different way. You don't need to stay attached to your micro goals – you're free to switch them up, amend them or replace them with alternative methods any time you feel they're not serving you.

Development plans

Writing time: one hour, review every few weeks

Preparation: single sheet of paper and pen (or new Word document)

Recommended practice: one initial session to map out your plan, and then shorter review sessions to check in or make amendments

First up, what is a development plan? Simply put, this is a strategy to accelerate your personal growth. It's a goal-setting, progress-tracking, motivation-building tool. Essentially, it's a way to observe your own development. And there are no real rules about the specific details – you can tailor it to make it work for you. Here are the essential components.

First step

Get clear about what you want from the exercise. Take a few minutes to note down whatever comes to mind: career goals; passions and projects; family, community or social interests. What is it you really want to achieve? You might find that you completed much of this work in Chapter 3 – if so, you can use these notes as your foundation for this exercise.

You can, of course, have different development plans for different goals (for example: one for work; one for relationships, etc.). Or you can weave a couple of main goals into a single plan. But for the purpose of this exercise, we're going to stick with the idea of a single overarching goal.

Second step

Once you have a sense of your goal, break it down into manageable steps. For example, if your goal is to excel in your career, your manageable steps could look something like this:

1.   research specific types of employment;
2.   reach out to professionals who work in those areas of employment;
3.   build mentoring relationships with those individuals;
4.   apply for internships, work experience or other opportunities in those fields.

It doesn't need to be exact – the idea is just to split up the overall goal into a number of specific stages.

Third step

After you create your list, revisit it. Go back through the list, checking to see which items should be given the highest priority. If you're finding it difficult to prioritize, it could be because your steps aren't specific or tangible enough – you might need to break them down even further to create your personal development plan.

Fourth step

Once you have your list, turn them from theoretical steps into practical actions. Let's say your step is: '*research specific areas of employment*'. You can turn this into an action by figuring out *when* you'll do it, *how* you'll go about it and *what* resources you need to get you there. For example:

> On Monday afternoon at 3 pm, I will spend two hours researching specific areas of employment, using Google search, library resources and careers service advice. After researching, I will record my findings, including any relevant details (for example, the skill-set needed to excel in this area of employment).

Fifth step

The next step is to develop a timeline. Your timeline could be driven by external events (for example, application deadlines), or you could set yourself a personal target and see how fast you can meet it. Either way, the important thing is to set a concrete deadline, and make sure you check in with yourself at that point. If it's just a personal target, you don't necessarily need to have finalized the goal by the deadline: you can always realign your expectations of timing. As long as you're making consistent, good-quality progress in your desired direction, that's still a win.

Final step

Your personal development plan should include a way to track your own development, whether it's a reminder for self-reflection, or a reminder to obtain feedback from other people (or both). You can choose how to record your findings – bullet points, a narrative journal-style entry, keywords… play around with different strategies, and figure out what works best for you.

For all of these steps, the important thing is not the specific format (you're free to tailor that for yourself), but the *consistency* with which you engage with the plan. The most successful outcomes (as for most of the exercises in this book) will result from careful planning, well-paced execution and a steady sense of motivation.

Milestone mapping

Writing time: 15 minutes to map out

Preparation: your choice of calendar or diary

Recommended practice: one initial session to map out your milestones, and then designing a way to recognize your achievement when you reach them

This is a simple exercise that focuses on the power of celebration. We often forget, as we race towards bigger and bigger goals, that there's an immense psychological power in taking a moment to appreciate where we are right now. We've all heard about the power of the gratitude journal, and perhaps you've experienced it too – the positive impact that can result from something as simple as noting the things you're grateful for. 'Milestone mapping' is a similar psychological strategy: it encourages you to reach a goal, and then take a second to pause and appreciate it.

It's been reported that focusing on a positive experience takes a consistent amount of focus and intention, while focusing on negative experiences is much more instinctive.[10] So, with this in mind, the milestone mapping exercise is based on the following steps:

1. *Choose your milestone.* It's up to you whether you want to make this is a big goal (a macro-style goal, if you're using the goal-setting exercise above – see pp. 96–102) or a smaller, more achievable goal. It might even make sense to have smaller markers for your mini-milestones and a bigger marker for your main, macro goal.

2. *Mark your milestone in your planner of choice* – perhaps the calendar app on your phone, a paper diary or other tracking method. It might be, for example, the day of a final exam or the day of launch of a project. You can choose whether to mark the milestone on that particular day (which might work in the exam example) or the day/week after (which might be more appropriate for a new project, since the immediate aftermath of the launch might still involve a large amount of work).

3. *Decide what your celebration or marker will look like.* You can get a little creative here: it might be something low-intensity (like having a few days off to do your favourite things or

---

[10] For example: https://econtent.hogrefe.com/doi/10.1027/1618-3169/a000124

catch up on Netflix), or something more significant (taking a vacation or having a gathering of friends and family). You can even craft something personalized to the particular milestone – for example, finishing an exam might mean you have a celebratory evening with your classmates, or getting a promotion might mean spending on something meaningful for yourself. Whatever it is, make sure it's designed in some detail: this will not only serve as your milestone (i.e. your memory of achievement), but as an incentive to reach the milestone.

One important part of this practice is to create a record of the event in some way. So, for example, if it's a post-exam gathering, take photos and keep them. If you decide to invest in a product or item, make it something that lasts. You want to keep associating the positive experience of the milestone with the achievement of the event itself. It's strange how our minds work – the more we tell ourselves stories about the things that happened to us, the more they can become our defining memory of those things. Our perception is malleable, and we can use that to our advantage in encouraging positive reflections on a particular experience (even if the experience itself was difficult).

Checklist creation

Writing time: 30 minutes

Preparation: Word document

Recommended practice: 30 minutes to define and create your checklists, then return every week and adjust as necessary

I'll be honest with you: this one is my favourite. For me, checklists have always been the most effective way of staying on top of my goals (and life), and keeping 'checked in' to the path I'm taking. It's been said many times (and originally attributed to writer Will Durant, summarizing Aristotle), but 'we are what we repeatedly do'. Our everyday actions, no matter how small and inconsequential they seem, add up. Over time, they result not only in the shape and design of our lives, but the shape and design of our *selves*. Without sounding too dramatic, they make us who we are.

This is where the checklist strategy comes in. Checklists are an immensely efficient way of staying on top of where you are in the world, because they can be designed to fit your exact specifications. If you've already done the difficult work of Chapter 3 (figuring out where your purpose might lie, or what your path might look like), you can make the work into an actionable step by bringing it into a checklist format. You can also integrate checklists with other strategies in this chapter – for example, the goal-setting strategy or a development plan.

Here are the key components of your checklist:

1. a set of actionable steps – practically formulated (rather than being broad, abstract or theoretical);
2. orientated towards a measurable, purposeful goal (rather than being vague or having no meaning to you); and
3. in an order that serves a purpose (rather than being scattered or unclear).

With those overarching principles in mind, you can start to design your own checklist.

First step

Get clear, in detail, about the intention of your checklist. Checklists are best used for smaller goals, since a checklist should be completed in a fairly short timeframe (think daily or weekly checklists, rather than annual). And the goal should be practical – instead of something like: 'be a more compassionate person', think more along the lines of: 'develop habits of compassion and empathy to demonstrate every day to the people around me'.

Of course, the checklist doesn't have to be personality-based: you can use checklists for a wide range of things you want to achieve, from gaining a new set of skills (checklists for revision, practice, research and execution) to simply getting things done (checklists for completion, output and projects).

You can have a couple of checklists running at one time – for example, a daily checklist to help you execute your study goals, and a weekly checklist to check in on your fitness goals – but I'd recommend not to expand the number of checklists you run in parallel beyond three or four. The more places for you to focus your attention, the less you have available for the efficient execution of the things that matter most, so it pays to prioritize.

Second step

Once you have your goal, reverse-engineer it to get your steps. This is a similar process to the one you might have gone through in the goal-setting strategy at the start of this chapter (see pp. 96–102). You're looking for a number of steps in the range of 5–10 – more than this can get a little complex, and fewer than this might suggest you need a different method (try the goal-setting strategy, or a development plan – see pp. 96–102 and pp. 102–106).

Once you have your set of steps, check each one to make sure it adheres to the following principles, as outlined above:

1. The steps should be *actionable* – is it clear to you which action each step demands?

2. The steps should be *purposeful* – is it clear to you what you're trying to achieve?

3. The steps are *logical* – are they in the right order? Does anything need to be added or subtracted? Could any of the steps be combined?

Third step

Test-drive the checklist a few times, refining and realigning each time as appropriate. Don't expect that your checklist will operate perfectly on the first few tries – after all, you've created the checklist in the abstract, and its practical application can be very different. It's also helpful not to be too attached to any particular steps. If they're not serving you, swap them out for something else. As much as possible, try and find some metrics by which to measure your success, and make sure that your checklist is orientating you in the desired direction.

All these steps are possible even for checklists that are working on broader character traits, rather than specific daily tasks. Using the example above, if you were working on a checklist to encourage compassion in your daily life, you can measure this by assessing your interactions with others, asking for feedback or doing some other kind of self-awareness exercise (journaling, structured conversations with friends or family, meditation, and so on).

If, after some time has passed, your checklist becomes redundant (perhaps because the steps of the checklist become ingrained, instinctive habits) or unhelpful (perhaps because the steps are not delivering the results they were designed for), take the opportunity to revise and restructure – or replace it altogether.

The end goal is either to achieve the thing you wanted, if it's a single one-time achievement, or to let the steps of the checklist become a natural habit, if it's an ongoing goal or ambition. So, notice when you might need to make adjustments.

Personal branding

Writing time: weekly sessions of 20–30 minutes

Preparation: portfolio or notebook

Recommended practice: take a longer session to complete your initial reflections, and then return regularly to update and amend as appropriate

The idea of personal branding has always sounded a little forced to me. It seems unnatural to make yourself into a 'brand', and it also reflects a world where we see ourselves as 'products', rather than human beings. But, as participants in that world, it helps to have a handle on what personal branding actually *is*, and master some basic tools you can use to your advantage whenever you do have to project yourself in an external way.

First step

Personal branding works best when you have an idea of what you want to get out of the process, so get clear on what this personal branding exercise is *for*. Is it to build your reputation in your career, or step into a new industry? Or perhaps you're just trying to get a sense of where you're at right now, or the kind of external image you've built in your life and work so far.

You can get a little more clarity about the purpose of the exercise by answering the following questions:

1. Who is the recipient of your personal brand? Who is receiving your output and contribution to the world? Who does your work serve?
2. What kind of impact do you want your personal brand to have? What kind of emotion, perspective or attitude do you want to leave the recipient with?
3. If you could just have a totally private personal brand, would it still matter to you? Are you

designing with external intention, or are you purely undertaking this exercise for yourself?

There are no right or wrong answers here, just an insight into your motivation and desired outcomes.

Second step

Gather as much information as you can for the following categories:

1. How do other people see you in the world? How would they describe you? Does this correspond to your own views and opinions of yourself?
2. What would other people say your mission or purpose is? Does this correspond to your own views and opinions of yourself?
3. If you could design your own ideal personal brand – in just a few sentences – what would you want it to incorporate?
4. What would you want people to be saying about you when you're not around? Does that correspond with what you think they're saying about you in reality?
5. If you were to try and assess your path so far from an external perspective, what would your personal brand look like? Think about it from the perspective of a recruiter, or someone who has come across you online. What would they

say? What opinions or assumptions would they draw?

6. Looking at all of your social media accounts or other online profiles, repeat the exercise under no. 5 above.

7. Looking at the results of a Google search of your name, repeat the exercise under no. 5 above.

Third step

Using your findings from the steps above, map out your existing personal brand. Here are a couple of format ideas you can use to write it out:

1. *An author bio.* Take a look at the biographies of your favourite authors on the back of their books (maybe even use this book!) and see if you can craft your own author bio using your information from the personal branding exercise above. In terms of content, you can include anything that feels relevant. You're just trying to emulate the style (and most importantly, the length) of a typical author bio.

2. *A social media bio.* Even shorter than the author bio: the social media bio. Take a look at some people who inspire you online, and see what they say about themselves. The restriction to a certain number of lines and characters

normally makes people draw out the most important aspects of themselves.

3. *A CV summary*. Even if you don't currently need one, draft yourself a short CV summary. This should be 3–4 lines long and brief enough to fit in the header of a CV template. Again, the content is up to you – it doesn't have to be totally work-related.

Fourth step

Once you've played around with the formats and drafted your *current* personal branding summary, take a pen in another colour, and revisit. Go back through the text and mark whenever you encounter something that you want to change or improve. You could either replace the current text with something that fits your goals more closely, or you can simply highlight or underline the elements you want to amend. In this way, you get a simple visual representation of the things you want to change, and a sense of how you want to change them.

Final step

If this process gives rise to inspiration or new ideas, you know what to do – use one of the other tracking or goal-orientated methods in this book (try the goal-setting exercise from this chapter, or the dream

CV exercise in Chapter 3: see pp. 96–102 and pp. 80–84) to add in your new ambitions, ideas and concepts.

(*A final note*: the key to many of these purpose-finding practices is to take the final step and make them a part of your practical, day-to-day life. We often think we find change through moments of revelation and external inspiration, but the reality is – for most of us – that long-lasting change tends to come through daily, persistent, practical steps that alter the course of our lives and selves.)

A QUICK NOTE ON WHERE WE'RE AT

This chapter finishes up the main purpose-focused exercises of the book. Chapters 5, 6 and 7 take you through the frameworks that will support you on your path: the power of practice, the importance of networks, and the foundations of wellbeing.

But, as you move forwards, the work you've already completed in Chapters 3 and 4 will be of fundamental importance. The insights from the exercises will guide you in the right direction, towards your personal sense of purpose. Next, we'll look at how you'll make the journey your own.

CHAPTER 5

THE PRACTICE OF PURPOSE

Developing a rhythm to your life

By now, you're (hopefully!) starting to see a bit of clarity when it comes to figuring out who you are, and what you're supposed to be doing with your life. But, as with most meaningful changes, the process of 'finding a sense of purpose' is continually evolving. This chapter will help you build your foundations for a purpose-driven lifestyle, setting up habits and practices to keep yourself on the right track as your life – and purpose – develops.

The thing about self-help books

Self-help has a bad reputation. If you think of self-help, you might end up imagining someone who is hooked on 'motivational quotes', or stuck in a cycle of self-improvement without ever making a real difference in their lives. But 'self-help', defined broadly, actually has a long and impressive history. In fact, it's possible to classify a lot of philosophy or theology as 'help for the self', if you think about what it's designed to do (for example, the work of Epicurus, or Seneca).

So, the problem with self-help books is not with their intention, or the fact that they could be attributed to a passing trend. The problem with self-help books, in many cases, is that they present you with a fixed solution to a defined issue.

Think about the first self-help book that comes to mind. Of course, not all self-help books will fit this template, but there's a good chance that the book follows this format:

1. Problem
2. Consequences
3. Proposed solution

I've read enough self-help books to know that this actually *works*, in some cases. Maybe there really is a straightforward problem, for which there's a solution you haven't tried yet, and the book gives you a simple way to implement it. Perfect, and worth your investment. But when it comes to something as complex and integrated and evolving and – well – *messy* as your life, a different strategy is required.

Instead of offering a fixed solution, you'll have seen that the previous chapters offer a variety of methods, to be worked through in your own time and integrated into your lifestyle in the way that feels most appropriate. This chapter moves on to the practical question of how you *reshape* your life around the findings from the purpose-orientated work you've completed.

It's your life, after all

Let's start with a simple exercise. Take a step into the future (let's say five years from now) and look back at your life. Take a brief snapshot of your life in the present moment: your friends, relationships, family members; your home, job and career; your skill-set, goals and ambitions; your body and your mind and your soul. How are you feeling about it, in general? Are you settled? At peace with your past? At home in your body?

The purpose of this exercise, at this point, is not to complete another written reflection, or even to 'discover' anything specifically. It's just to take a quick overview of what you're dealing with, so you can pick and mix from the rest of the activities in this chapter, in order to select the ones that would fit well into your life, and skip over the ones that wouldn't.

When I was younger, whenever we went to a café, I'd always choose the same thing to eat: 'Five Things In A Box' (I'm pretty sure this still exists – I hope it does). The thing I *loved* about this was the act of choosing five food items, totally individual to me, and putting them together as a selection in a box. Maybe it comes back to this idea of finding your own sense of structure in an otherwise chaotic universe – the art of intentional design, amongst all the possible choices of things that could happen. Anyway, this is a 'Five Things In A Box' chapter. The practices below are yours to pick and choose from – try a few out, keep the ones that resonate and leave the ones that don't. Come back to the full selection often, just in case you want to swap one out or add one in or amend your choices. These small, almost-imperceptible actions are the steps to designing the life you want.

Tracking your days

There are a couple of methods for tracking your days, but let's start with a general overview of what this technique is intended to achieve. Tracking your days is a great way to develop a sense of *awareness* – the ability to observe your life as it develops. You might find it's also easier to get a sense of your own story (recall the narrative-development exercise from Chapter 3, pp. 55–62) if you're reflecting on your days over time.

What it's *not* intended to do is make you feel trapped in your own life, or like you need to stick to a specific template for your days, or that you've failed (or succeeded) if your days look a certain way. It's a flexible method, one that can be picked up and put down at various times. For example, during a particularly busy period at work or in your personal life, you might find it helpful to pause your tracking or self-development practices. Or, you might find it even more helpful to step up your practices during that time, as a support mechanism. The choice is all yours, depending on how it feels and how it works, in practice, within your life.

The other thing to notice, over time, is whether a specific practice is actually serving you. As with the other options discussed in this chapter, I'd encourage you to be critical when it comes to adopting new habits, routines and rituals into your days. You don't need to be doing things that don't actually serve a purpose (unless you want to be doing them). If it feels unduly stressful trying to track your days using any of these methods, *and* if you feel like this pressure is not outweighed by any tangible benefit, swap the practice out for something else.

As you may have noticed by now, there's a bit of a theme developing in this book – the theme of unique life design and structure, according to *your* specifications. You can think of it like building or designing a house to live in: there might be some consistent design and structural features that fit your ideals over time, but you're going to want different sizes, locations and interior design as you change and evolve and grow. So, try things, listen carefully to your life to see what the feedback is, and then adjust and respond accordingly.

Method 1: time tracking

This method works best if *either* (1) you want to get a good sense of how your time is being spent across your days or weeks, *or* (2) you want to observe how you spend time on different activities. If you're fairly settled with the way your days are structured, skip to Method 2 or 3. But for the rest of us, this is how you can begin to track your time.

First, figure out whether you want to do it the old-school way (pen and paper) or via an app or digital notepad. This makes a difference – not only psychologically (sometimes it's just more satisfying to have things down on paper), but also physically (because it determines whether or not you have your phone accessible during your day – something that might actually detract from your productivity levels).

Once you choose your option, work out what you're tracking. The extreme version of this method might be to track every activity, mapping out your entire day from waking to sleeping. This might be a helpful exercise for a short-term project, to see what it is you actually focus your attention on, but it's unlikely to be helpful in the long term – it requires a lot of commitment, and it's probably the case that you spend more time perfecting the exercise than you do actually completing the work.

So, another option is to pick a certain activity to track, and focus on this for a certain period of time. This activity could be general (the topic of 'work', for example), or specific (a particular work project, for example). You can track hours, minutes or blocks of time – for example, a morning, afternoon or evening slot. During this exercise, you're not necessarily tracking to meet particular targets. It's more an exercise of observation: figuring out how you spend your time. After completing the exercise over a week or so, you can look back and reassess. Are your hours going towards the most important things, or are there some priorities that need to be shifted?

An example of time tracking over the period of a week might look something like this (I'll use the example of 'Project A' as the thing to track):

MONDAY:

Afternoon: 4 hours Project A

TUESDAY:

Morning: 1 hour Project A

Evening: 1 hour Project A

THURSDAY:

Afternoon: 4 hours Project A

FRIDAY:

Evening: 1 hour Project A

Even from a rough outline of where the time is allocated over the course of the week, you can begin to develop a greater sense of awareness about your choices. In the example above, you can see that Monday and Thursday look better for 'deep work'[11] (where you might have a longer period of time in which to delve into a project on a focused level). Tuesday and Friday look a bit more broken up, so they might be good days to work on high-level details of the project. Wednesday and the weekend don't feature, so maybe that tells you to avoid relying on those time periods to complete Project A's tasks or deadlines – or maybe it tells you that you could reallocate project time to those days. This is your exercise, so only you will know what the results are telling you – and you're then free to make informed choices with that knowledge.

Method 2: habit tracking

It's likely you've heard a lot about habits – their power, their utility and their importance in your life. This is a method that encourages you to track them, either

---

[11] A concept popularized and developed by professor and author Cal Newport: www.calnewport.com/about/

to stop or start a habit, or to readjust, reorientate or realign an existing habit.

The first step, as with Method 1, is to pick your medium. It might be that the old-school option is the best – you can make a simple habit chart for yourself on a piece of paper (try making a table with the days of the week on the X axis and the number of times a certain habit is repeated on the Y axis). For this topic, however, there are a number of great habit-tracking apps out there. Since habit-tracking is a fairly straight-forward method, it might help to try out a few of the apps – you don't have to input details about your habit (you can always keep those offline), but it can be easier to track completion or non-completion of a habit in a simple electronic format. You can also choose whether to turn notifications on or off.

Once you've chosen your way of tracking, decide how many habits to track, and which kinds of habits. In some ways, our whole lives are comprised of small habits, so be specific about the ones you want to observe or amend. I'd recommend starting with no more than five habits to track (you can always work your way up to a higher number if it turns out to be an effective method for you). Some good examples include:

1. Meditation practice
2. Drinking water
3. Stretching or exercise

4. Journaling
5. Gratitude practices
6. Communication (for example, reaching out to friends, family or networks)
7. Giving someone a compliment
8. Working on a passion project
9. Moments of silence
10. Taking a walk outside

If you wanted to subdivide further, creating categories of items to track, you could split it into:

1. Mind
2. Body
3. Self
4. Work
5. Other

Of course, you should personalize and recategorize as you see fit.

Method 3: life mapping

The final method comes back to this idea of finding rhythm to your life. One of the greatest shifts in our generation has been a lack of structure to our overall year. Think of a traditional year 70 years ago: you might have shaped your week around family events, spiritual observances and the traditional working week. Going back even further, our days were determined by external factors: the time of the sunrise and sunset; the seasons of the year; the background and social classes we were born into.

Of course, these things still exist, but – in general – we live with more independence. We can get up when it's dark, or stay awake long after the sun sets. We can often shape our work and career choices independently of what our parents and grandparents ended up doing. But with all that choice, we can start to feel unanchored. Without structure, it can be easy to get lost.

One option is to pre-plan your year according to what you want to do or achieve. For that approach, I'd recommend adopting one or more of the exercises in Chapter 4 – these are designed to help you align with your goals and map out a lifestyle that works for you. But in this chapter, you can try a different approach. This is about *observing*, and then *reflecting* on that observation. This is also a longer-term method, so works best if you're looking for slow, consistent results.

Again, start by choosing your medium. For this method, I'd recommend the old-school way – perhaps an A3 sheet of paper, or a journal, or a portfolio-style book. At the end of each week, just make a simple note about what the general sense of the week was – a slower week, or higher-energy, or stressful, or externally focused (lots of meetings, communication, interactions) or internally focused (lots of thinking time, reflections, stillness). You can choose your own ways to categorize – you could even use colours, images or designs. The intention is not to control anything, but just to map out the narrative.

There are a couple of benefits to this approach:

- *first*, it gives your life a sense of structure and direction – you might be able to use the information in deciding what to do next, or when it comes to making decisions about how to spend your time or energy; and
- *second*, it enables you to see the evolution of your self and your life over time – almost an autobiographical function. It's not necessarily creating depth where there wasn't any before, but it is *showing* you things that you might have overlooked. It's easy to skim through life on the surface of our experiences. This exercise gives you an opportunity to reclaim it all; to make it part of your story – to award your time the quality that it deserves.

The purpose pause

Picking up on that sense of depth and quality, this next exercise is a simple daily practice to bring you back into the present moment. Hopefully, the tools in Chapters 3 and 4 have given you a sense of what you want to do with your life: the things that matter to you, and where you want to be directing your energy.

But even with the best of intentions, we can so easily get swept up in the demands of daily life. Sometimes it feels like we take our eye off the ball for a few seconds and wake up a few years later, wondering what exactly it was that we did with our time.

So this practice, while simple, is actually an act of rebellion. It's a push-back against the steady acceleration of culture, both in our working and personal lives. It's a way to reconnect, and you can carry it with you and deploy it at any time. I'm calling it 'The Purpose Pause'. Here are the steps.

First step

Notice. This is always the first step in an awareness or meditation-based practice: the simple act of noticing what's going on. Sometimes we catch ourselves on the wrong path – maybe we notice we've been scrolling pointlessly for a while, or we've diverted our attention away from our goal by accident – and we're annoyed about it. The annoyance – though understandable – is misplaced. This is because the *noticing* (the moment of awareness) is actually the key to returning to your path.

Our whole lives are an ebb and flow of movement. We lean into certain things, we orient our paths in a certain way, and then we forget and fall off track. We decide to start again, but slip back into old habits. We have a few weeks off. We return with a new focus. Whenever I work with meditation students, I try to encourage them to lean into this pattern. Instead of fighting to remain in a place of perfection, find the value in *noticing* when you came off track. The *noticing* element is helpful, not something to be handled with hostility. The first step is always noticing, and the choice of response can follow.

Second step

Move your environment. Sometimes the physical shifting of environment can have a profound impact on our internal thoughts, feelings and emotions. Try moving to another room of your house, or even stand up and stretch. If you find it effective, you can have a brief clean-up of your desk or your working environment. There's a reason that new starts often accompany a new image or a change of scene – we're visual creatures, and a change of environment often encourages a change on a deeper level of the psyche.

Third step

Bring your awareness into your body. A simple way to do this is to ground both of your feet on the floor, and focus all of your awareness and attention into the soles of your feet. An alternative option might be to place one hand on your heart centre and the other on your abdomen, with the palms facing inwards. A third option might be to place your hands on your knees or thighs, with the palms facing down. If you take either of the last two options, think about bringing your attention or awareness to the palms of your hands. Then, run through a quick checklist of questions:

1. How do I feel in my body, right now?
2. How do I feel emotionally, right now?
3. How do I feel in my mind, right now?

The 'emotionally'-focused question is a good one to fit in between body and mind, because it often bridges the gap between the two: emotions might originate in the mind and manifest in the body, or the other way round. It's also helpful to begin this practice with a body focus first, because it's often (although not always) easier to sense feelings on a physical level than it is to untangle the layers of thoughts in our minds.

If you don't get any specific answers to the questions, that's fine – at this stage, we're just taking a general check-in. The whole step should only take a few minutes. If you're finding there's more to explore, you can always extend the practice into a longer, body-focused meditation (see Chapter 7 for more on that).

Final step

This is where you tie it back to the question of purpose. It doesn't have to be your overall 'life purpose' – as you'll have learned throughout Chapter 3, this is a much bigger and more flexible question that you'll get to define (and redefine!) over time. But bring your-self back to your purpose *in this moment*. This might mean refocusing your attention on the task at hand, or it might mean reconnecting with your body, or anything else that feels like it's your purpose in the next hour or so of your day. This practice might give rise to a thought (for example, a reminder that you need to call someone or follow up on a task) – you can always make a quick note of that and then return to this place of pause.

To focus your attention, you can ask yourself the question:

What is purposeful for me, right now?

Or, more straightforwardly:

What is my purpose in this moment?

This is, in some ways, a mini-meditation, so it might help to keep your eyes closed (if that feels comfort-able), or deepen your breath, or integrate another meditative technique that helps you to focus. But you might prefer instead to make it more of a personal development exercise – maybe make a few notes about your experience, or use the moment of 'pause' to organize your materials for the next task on your list. It will probably be the case that different times of your life and your day will require different tech-niques. As with all of the exercises in this book, the most important thing is that they work to fit you (and not the other way around).

The importance of silence

You might remember the idea of the 'Rule of Life' exercise from Chapter 3: a set of guidelines and principles that you can use to restructure your days (see pp. 49–52). In my own experience of the 'Rule of Life' in practice, during my time on a monastic programme, one of the most memorable 'rules' was *Silence*. This was broadly described as follows:

> Silence is the absence of noise, silence is the quietness of the heart, silence is discipline in speech, silence is reflection, silence is being present in the 'now'.

You've probably experienced a variety of silences in your life. There are beautiful moments of stillness, perhaps in nature or alone. There are quiet moments of reflection, of emotion, of hope or grief or despair. There are silences during conversations; meaningful pauses; silences that demonstrate closeness or distance between people. There are silences that make you wonder what's coming next, or give you an opportunity to find clarity and peace.

I don't think we get enough silence in our world. Think of the last time you comfortably sat or rested in silence, alone with your thoughts. I'm sure I'm not the only one who has background music or a podcast playing in the quieter moments of my day. Silence can be scary, because it leaves us alone with the present moment – it makes us face up to what's happening right now, both around us and within us. But it can also be powerful. Those who are able to use silence as a tool, to sit quietly with themselves, are likely to be those who find the focus and discipline to stay on their path, even when the world pushes them in a different direction. It takes strength of character to choose silence over the noise of social media and email notifications, and it takes courage to *remain* there, in a place of silence, letting your own thoughts settle.

A quick note about silence in the mental health context. If you're someone with a strong or forceful inner voice, silence is not always helpful. It might actually be that silence is more difficult or challenging than having a structured conversation with someone. Similarly, for those undergoing a difficult life event – like a loss or a sudden transition – silence can be immensely painful. It might be helpful to speak to a therapist or other qualified mental health professional if you feel challenged by the idea of silence – if nothing else, it might help you to clarify some of your own thoughts and emotions around the topic.

But, if you're ready, let's dive into the topic of silence. This section will offer you a number of ways to encourage silence into your life.

Pockets of silence

Let's start small. If you're used to filling your day with noise and activity, your first challenge is to find *three* pockets of silence within your day. It doesn't matter when they are, but claim them for yourself. You can always make a note of when they happen during the initial days of practising, if helpful – it might give you an indication of when to look out for them in the future.

Some examples might be:

- first thing in the morning;
- last thing in the evening;
- transitions between tasks or projects;
- after or before phone calls;
- after or before you check your emails;
- the first few moments of walking;
- queuing to get into a shop or café; or
- just before you join a meeting.

The pocket only needs to be a few minutes long, but recognize that you're claiming it – own it for yourself, and notice what it feels like to be in it. Some of the examples above might be easier than others – for example, when you're out walking, it's much easier to be in silence, since the external environment 'supports' you with its own activity and noise. The hardest moments might be first thing in the morning, or transitioning between tasks and projects. See if you can challenge yourself with a few simple pockets of silence and a few more difficult ones.

Days of silence

In this step, we're moving up to the next level. After practising pockets of silence for some time, you might want to experiment with a day of silence. Importantly, this doesn't mean you have to spend the entire day not speaking. This is just the 'theme' of your day: it means that you *choose* silence whenever you have a choice. So, for example, it means not filling gaps in your day with noise and activity, but instead choosing to do your daily tasks in silence. During my monastic training, our silent days sometimes involved things like teaching or spoken prayer – so we weren't totally silent to the point of strictness, but instead just abiding by the principle of 'silence first'.

To make this easier, you can always get yourself an accountability partner – perhaps someone you live with, or you could check in with a friend throughout the day via text or email. My recommendation would be to treat this exercise with lightness – you don't have to stick to silence if it's necessary to speak. This is just an experiment to see what it would be like to theme your day around a singular principle. You might even expand it out to cover the course of a week (see below).

One other thing: as with many of the exercises in this book, it's helpful to do a little self-observation. Figure out what it felt like to have a silence-themed day and notice any changes in yourself going forwards. What did you struggle with? What did you enjoy? Anything you want to take forward as information or insights to help you shape your life?

Silent retreats

The final practice in this section is the 'silent retreat'. This sounds a little intimidating (and, as someone who has been on a couple of silent retreats, it actually *is* a little intimidating). But, as with the 'silent days' practice above, we're going to keep it light. This is your own mini-retreat, and it can be done from the comfort of your own home, without leaving your life behind.

Start by allocating your week for the retreat. In practice, silent retreats are often longer than a week – ten days might be a traditional measure of time in some settings, or even longer, to really settle in. But, for your first personal silent retreat, a week is a helpful measure of time: a Monday to Sunday pattern gives you a structure to follow, and it seems fairly attainable.

Then, set yourself some retreat practices. Maybe you'll just extend the principle of 'silence first' into a week. Perhaps you'll add in a few structured meditation practices, or pockets of silence. You can get creative here: you could do a week of silent mornings or evenings, and see if you can structure your main meetings and other obligations around this. You could pause your social interactions for a week, or try and keep them to a minimum. You could keep a disciplined journal for a week, noticing the impact that silence has on yourself and your life. Design your retreat however you want, and remember that you can adjust or amend your practices as you go through – as long as you try not to abandon the retreat halfway through.

After you set out the content and themes of your retreat, design an opening and closing practice for yourself. In traditional retreat settings, there is often a ritual that opens and closes the retreat, and the psychological impact of having a pattern to shape the opening and closing of the space is significant. For you, this might be something like an extended meditation, or clearing out your physical space, or starting and finishing a new journal. You can make your start and close ritual as elaborate and personal as you like. And even if it feels unnecessary, I'd encourage you to give it a go. There's a reason that ritual and ceremony has been a part of our culture for thousands of years: it's powerful, and it can take you into a place of openness and preparedness that you might not have reached otherwise.

The final step is to set up some backup plans. Go through the possible triggers that might make you want to quit halfway through: a midweek slump in energy, the new release of a TV series, a friend wanting to chat, a social event, etc. Next to each trigger, note down – with specificity – what you'll do when it happens. Be detailed with your answers – note down how you'll respond, what actions you'll take, and the steps you'll follow to get yourself back to your original intention. Keep this somewhere you can refer to it. Distractions aren't just a possibility, they're an inevitability, so it's helpful to have a practical plan of action. (As a side-note, I was distracted countless times during silent retreat, even in a monastic community in the middle of the countryside with little phone signal – so it's always good to anticipate things ahead of time.)

Words, themes, affirmations and mantras

We won't spend too long on this section – largely because a lot of this content is covered in more specific books on personal development, but also because I tend to use these categories as an add-on to my substantive purpose-focused practices, rather than the foundation of my work. (That's not to say I don't find these practices effective or powerful, but I generally think they work well when you've *already* done the difficult work of figuring your life out.) So, we'll be finishing off the chapter with this section, and then we'll move on to the more practical, day-to-day side of your purpose-focused work.

Words and themes

In the sections above, we covered the idea of shaping your life – through practices like tracking your days or pausing to refocus your purpose. This is another method to give some shape to the course of your life: choosing a word or a theme.

This is an interesting approach, because words and phrases can sometimes *create* thoughts or emotions where they weren't there before. They can also some-times name something with such precision that it calls out a previously-unknown part of our beliefs or self.

With that in mind, this exercise is simple. Give each week a word or a theme that focuses the time and aligns it to your goals and ambitions.

(*A side note*: you'll see here how important it is that you already did the difficult work of Chapters 3 and 4 – this exercise is just capturing that work in an action-able format.)

Some examples might be:

- Ambition
- Empathy
- Compassion

- Awareness
- Presence
- Motivation
- Achievement
- Humility

To select a phrase, you could either combine a few single words that feel appropriate (for example: ambition, motivation and achievement), or you can craft an action-based statement for your week. Some examples of the latter might be:

- I will enter this week with a sense of calm purpose.
- I will remain present and grounded this week, regardless of the challenges.
- I will retain my sense of motivation this week, and complete my projects with a sense of ownership.

Again, feel free to shape these words and statements however you like.

One other option for using this technique is to start a one-line journaling practice. This normally consists of writing just one line per day, but you can use your word or theme of the week to structure your thoughts. For example, your prompt line could be:

1. How would I describe today in a single sentence?
2. What went well today?

3. How am I feeling today?
4. What did I learn today?
5. What do I want from tomorrow?

To integrate this single-line journaling exercise with your word or theme, write down your word or theme as a header, and then start your single-line journaling in alignment with that word or theme. For example:

WORD: AMBITION

How would I describe today in a single sentence?

Today, I was clear about my ambitions at work and articulated them well within my team meeting.

Affirmations and mantras

As above, I'd generally encourage you to use these as add-ons or anchors to your main purpose-finding practices – but, as always, you can assess how helpful they are for you in practice. Affirmations and mantras tend to be a little on the 'spiritual' side for those who prefer a clear personal development practice, but stay open-minded: you might find they help to keep you on track.

First, a quick definition:

> *Affirmations* are statements of assertion, typically phrased with a positive orientation. For example: 'I am capable and motivated', or 'I am creative and purpose-driven'.

> *Mantras* (from Sanskrit, with its root sometimes translated as 'vehicle') are words or phrases that are repeated consistently – either during the course of a traditional meditation or yoga practice, or as part of a personal development practice. They don't have to be positively phrased or focused on the self, but you'll often see them formulated in that way. For example: 'I am here', or 'I am present in this moment'.

You might find it useful to start your week with an affirmation – perhaps write it down and display it somewhere, so you can check in during the week to see how things are going. Or, you might prefer to adopt a mantra each morning, and repeat it to yourself throughout the course of the day. Again, get creative – you can always pick and choose your affirmations or mantras to fit into other practices from this chapter, or from other chapters in this book.

CHAPTER 6

YOUR COMPASS

The support you can find around you

After the challenging, self-focused work of Chapters 3, 4 and 5, we're ready to turn our focus outwards. As much as purpose-finding is a personal journey, you don't have to make it alone. Setting up networks and support structures early on will help you to stay focused, grounded and intentional. And, of course, the relationships and connections you choose to develop will shape your own sense of purpose over time.

Your community

On a personal level, it wasn't until I started my monastic training programme that I really understood the value of community. Perhaps like you, I'd always been encouraged to follow my own path, working towards independence and self-sufficiency. But it was my monastic experience of being 'in community' with other people, working towards a shared goal or ambition, that introduced me to a new perspective. So, with that in mind, here are a few thoughts about the value of community, at a very high level. For more on issues of race, class and privilege, as these topics relate to community, check out the 'Resources' chapter.

An accepting community is often a fundamental part of feeling settled in the world

We all want to feel 'at home' in our own lives. Perhaps you've even experienced the opposite: the sense that you're not accepted in your own community or life. These emotions – the feeling of being 'at home', and the feeling of being rejected or unaccepted – have real, tangible, practical consequences for us. It's possible that we push against a feeling of rejection, seeking acceptance elsewhere, or retreating further into ourselves. Or perhaps we just continue our daily lives with a feeling that we don't really belong, or that we're not really fulfilling our full potential. This can have huge implications when it comes to doing personal purpose-focused work. In some cases, we're less likely to be in touch with our true intuitions, passions and sense of meaning if it's been shaped over the years by a sense of 'not belonging'.

A community built around a shared goal, ambition or mission has power

You might find that your fundamental support network (family, friends, etc.) is there for you, but that there's an absence of shared mission. This can be fairly subtle, but often is made manifest when it comes to choices about your purpose, and the way in which you want to design your life. Perhaps you feel that others don't understand or approve of your choices – even if it doesn't hold you back on a practical level, this factor can still be present in the decisions you make about what to do next. On the other hand, when you have a support system behind you that is aligned with your vision and mission, you've built some momentum before you've even started.

Your community doesn't all need to be from one place, or one 'type' of person

We're not necessarily talking about getting the support of a specific group of people, unless that's fundamentally important to you from a personal perspective. Instead, think about getting support from a wide variety of people and networks, all of whom will play a different but significant role in supporting you. Your support network, like your concept of purpose, will also evolve over time – you'll gain new members of

149

the network, move on from others and keep maintaining the relationships that matter. The more varied and diverse the community around you, the more creative, inspired and energized you're likely to become.

Your networks

What comes up when you read the phrase: 'the power of a network'? To me, it sounds like a LinkedIn headline, or a clickbait article convincing you to send unsolicited emails to people you barely know. Let's reframe that idea. Today's networks aren't just about what you can *obtain*, but also about what value you can *provide*. So, one important question to ask yourself at this point:

What value am I delivering to my network?

Since we're thinking about networks in a more 'holistic' way, you can consider personal elements as well as work-focused things. So, for example, you can think of the type of qualities you bring to relationships – things like compassion, generosity and kindness. Remember that it's not just the work you do in the world that matters, it's the person you are in the process of doing the work. In the end, this might just be the most important part of your purpose-orientated journey: not what you do, or what you receive, but who you *become* as a result of pursuing your path.

A brief network-focused exercise:

First, make a list of all the things you bring to the relationships with your network. You don't have to be specific about *who* the people are in your network (i.e. you don't have to name names, although you can if you find it helpful to focus your attention). Just think about the quality of your personal relationships in general. What type of person are you when it comes to interactions with others? Include as many examples as you can.

Next, make a list of all the things you *want* to bring to your relationships. Be as ambitious as you like here: include everything from personal qualities to character traits. You can cover things you already put down for the first step, if they belong on this list as well.

After this, work back through your second list and compare it to your first. Note the key qualities that appear on the second list but not on the first list. You can decide what to do with this information – it might be that some of the items on the list give you inspiration for the exercises you did in Chapters 3 and 4, and you might want to reassess your priorities as a result.

For example, if you end up with 'compassionate' on your second list but not on your first, you might want to set yourself a goal to develop more compassion in your everyday interactions with your community/network. In practice, this goal might look something like:

1. research the concept of compassion; obtain a general understanding of why it matters and how to develop it;
2. set yourself some practical challenges – maybe a daily reminder to demonstrate compassion in an interaction every day;
3. track your progress over time; obtain feedback from others if it's helpful; notice when people extend compassion to you and take notes on its impact.

Goals are certainly more difficult to set when it comes to personality development, rather than practical development (for example, completing a project). This is partly because 'completion' is never really final in this context – our personalities are fluid, and they develop over time. Traits like compassion, empathy, motivation, perseverance – these all need maintenance, and they're not one-time achievements. On the other hand, this should give you encouragement when it comes to figuring out who you want to be in the world: our personalities are, indeed, fluid – and you get to choose who to become.

Coming back to the question of value, start to reorientate your perspective to see things from other people's point of view. Think about the most important people in your network: the people you look up to, or idolize, or admire in some way. What kind of value are they delivering to you? What kind of value are you delivering to them? What kind of value arises from the relationship between both of you?

The last point is important, because it really touches on the heart of the importance of a network. It's not, in the end, just about you. And it's not just about them, either. Instead, it's about the power of both of you, working together, to create something that didn't previously exist: a *third thing*, that arises out of the power of the connection between you and others. This is what happens when you start to put your purpose-orientated work and vision out into the world: the value it delivers to other people becomes part of a broader structure, incorporating and integrating the value that other people are delivering to you.

Your audience

Your audience are the people who listen and consume and (sometimes) respond to your work in the world. They could be critics or fans – at this point, we're thinking in general terms. Your audience are the *recipients* – they're who your work is produced for.

This is a bit of a shift to the way we've been thinking about purpose so far, and it's worth spending a bit of time on it. Up to this point, we've been focused on purpose as a function and property of your own life: your own desires, wants, characteristics and preferences. But when it comes to the question of doing something *practical* with your purpose, we have other considerations. Purpose, as we've discovered, is a flexible concept, and it can be applied in different ways. So, when it comes to thinking about the impact your work might have in the world, you often have the ability to realign your purpose to fit the needs of your audience.

If this sounds a little complex, don't worry – it's actually more intuitive than it seems, and you've most likely been doing it already. Let's take an example.

In this example, we'll say that your current purpose, after doing the work in Chapters 3 and 4, is to demonstrate your creativity by putting your art into the world. Maybe you did a few goal-setting exercises and figured out that you want to feature in certain publications, or you filled up a dream CV with the awards and achievements you want to obtain. But let's think about *how* you might go about delivering that to the world.

One option might be to plough ahead with your inner vision, working solely on intuition and drive. Regardless of reviews and reception, you might choose to just put your work out there into the world – and this might deliver the goal you were hoping for. That's certainly one option, and if that works, great. But there's another way to approach this, a way that's more suited to the structure we're about to cover during this chapter. That's the idea of *co-creation* with the world, and specifically, with your audience.

Co-creation doesn't necessarily have to be a form of crowd-sourcing opinions, tailoring your output to feedback, or creating according to specific audience requests. Instead, co-creation can be as simple as figuring out what your audience wants, and delivering it to them – according to your own personal interpretation and style.

One final note about audience, before we move on. This section sounds a little like it only applies to people making creative work, or freelancers, or public figures, or people running businesses. That's not necessarily the case. The audience might be more easily identifiable in those cases, but we all have our audiences, and we all have our work in the world. If you're working within a large company, your work is anything you produce – projects, reports, presentations. If you're assisting others, your work is part of the final team product.

In fact, it's impossible (or at least, very difficult) to move through our lives without having some kind of impact on the people we encounter – whether through our work or anywhere else. Every interaction is, in some senses, our contribution to the world.

The risk is that we don't realize or pay attention to these elements, because we think they don't matter. But the truth is, it all matters – down to the smallest detail. This is the real gift of purpose-finding work: your whole life becomes the project. We start with a small focus (a job ambition; a career path; a relationship intention), and we move out to cover every aspect of our lives.

Your compass

So far, we've talked about community and networks, and we've covered (at a high level) the idea of having an audience for your work. This section will provide you with a visual way to conceptualize this: the compass image.

First up, a brief note – this is obviously not the only way to categorize things, and might not be the right way for you, either. I'd encourage you to try it out, see what it feels like: test whether it aligns with your life or not. And then, if not, take some of the ideas and make your own concept or diagram. There will be as many versions of this exercise as there are readers of this chapter, so make it unique and personal to you.

The compass image will take the four points we've covered so far:

1. You
2. Your community
3. Your network
4. Your audience

Here's a brief recap of each of those elements.

1. You

This is, of course, what most of this book has focused on so far, and you should have worked on a good starting point for yourself and your life in Chapters 3 and 4. We're now expanding the scope to cover not just yourself, but also...

2. Your community

Your community are the closest people around you – your family members, friends and others on your team. We spoke a little in the sections above about the importance of finding people who are aligned with your vision and helping you on your path. Of course, this might not always be possible, but I'd encourage you to keep the supportive members of your community close to you during the journey – they'll be a fundamental part of your structure when things get difficult. And, if you're lacking support amongst your closest community members, you can always expand your vision outwards to include...

3. Your network

Your network are the individuals within your scope, but with whom you might not be closest at this point. They could be colleagues, friends or peers – people you admire, or people who admire you, or people who have encountered your work. These individuals will be an important part in developing your support structure, and will no doubt play a part in shaping and influencing the course of your work.

And, finally, let's not forget who the work is actually *for*...

4. Your audience

Your audience are the consumers of your work: the people you create for, who will support and encourage and tell others about your work. This might be a digital audience, an international audience or a small group of customers or clients. To begin with, this group might be small – but, if you're doing important, impactful work that serves an existing need, it will grow.

Here's a diagram to help you map out all of this:

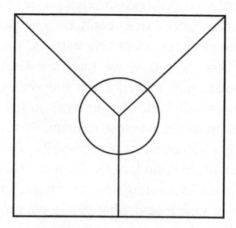

Breaking down your compass

You're at the centre – the circle. You form the consistent point between the three external segments, with an impact on each of them.

You can redesign this structure to match your understanding of your support system, but I'd suggest placing your community at the top. You can use the diagram to write in the names of some key members of your community, if that helps to crystallize the image in your mind.

The bottom two segments are your network and your audience. I generally think it works best to place these two elements side-by-side, rather than in a hierarchy. In an age where our networks are seamlessly blended into our audience through social media, and where our audience can so easily become part of our close networks after interacting with us, the boundaries are less clear than we imagine. Also, as you start to build up an audience – of supporters, clients, customers or recipients of your work in the world – it's important to remain close to them. By this I don't necessarily mean in terms of accessibility (we'll come on to the topic of boundaries in the next chapter), but in terms of understanding what they want, and allowing them to understand what you're offering. As we discussed above, you can start to think of this group of people as *co-creators* – people who receive your work, give their feedback on it and help you shape your output in a more effective, impactful way.

Two final points to note about this 'co-creation' concept. The first point is that this idea is receiving more attention as networks between communities, cultures and countries open up. We live in an international, globalized, diverse world – and the push towards more connection is clear, as our technology develops to facilitate it.

The second point is that this idea is anything but new. Human beings generally live in communities, and most of us have a natural instinct to care what other people think, and to adjust our behaviour and output because of it. This has good outcomes (making important work that matters) and less good outcomes (responding to group-think, peer pressure and crowd mentality). When it comes to our work, then, perhaps the best we can do is *notice* the impulse to respond to others, and make it an intentional part of the path we design for ourselves.

How to use your compass

Just like you would do with any compass (although I appreciate not many of us are regularly navigating our way around with one of those), you can use this concept to help you figure out your direction as you move through the world.

At some points, you'll turn towards your community for their thoughts and guidance. You'll often need to do this when faced with personal purpose-orientated questions. As we discussed in Chapters 3 and 4, your community can help when it comes to giving feedback on who you are at an intimate, individual level. They can also be a great way to turn when you need someone to cheer you on.

At other points, you'll turn to your networks. These people will be the source of support when it comes to things like references, referrals, testimonials, inspiration, mentoring and advice. You might have a couple of close members of your network who serve almost like a board of directors – a group of people you run your ideas past, to make sure you're on the right track.

Meanwhile, your audience will be the people to turn to when you put your work into the world. They'll be ready with feedback and thoughts and reviews, if you're making work that matters and that responds to a real need that they have.

You might have your own ideas of how these pieces fit together, but I'd encourage you to use the compass image as an intuitive tool.

What you're trying to do, in essence, is build a support *system* around you. Think of it less like a hierarchical ladder (your mentors above you; your mentees below you), and more like a holistic structure, allowing you to turn in whichever direction feels right. This process is, as with almost everything in life, informed by experience, mistakes and missteps. But this is your life, after all – you're the only one who can decide whether an approach worked or not, and the best strategy is to try things, listen, reflect, and then choose how to proceed.

CHAPTER 7

YOUR FOUNDATIONS

The fundamentals that enable you to live a purpose-driven life

By now, you should be equipped with some initial ideas about your purpose and what you want your life to look like. You might also have a good sense of your purpose-focused practices and habits, and an understanding of the people who will support you on the journey. But all of this is ineffective if you focus on purpose-finding to the exclusion of looking after yourself, on a very practical level.

So, this chapter gets into the practicalities. Thinking of purpose-finding as a part of your *existential wellbeing*, this chapter covers the other elements of 'being well'. I generally think of these elements as 'integrated' wellness: a blend of existential fulfilment (your purpose), mental health (your mind), physical health (your body), and a general feeling of being settled and grounded in the world.

And you'll see that the same principles come up repeatedly: intuitive awareness, embodiment, and a personalized approach. These core ideas can lay the foundations for a sustainable, fulfilling approach to wellness.

Your mind

It's been said that your thoughts determine your reality, and for good reason. We're starting here – with your mind – because it's from this place that change often begins. Knowing how to check in with yourself, how to understand your mind and how to respond when the pressure steps up: these will be the essential skills as you go about the difficult work of designing your life.

Mental health

Mental health: the basics

A broad definition of mental health usually includes psychological and emotional wellbeing. This is important, because mental health – even with the recent advances in openness and awareness when it comes to this topic – is often seen as an exclusively functional field: addressing the way you think so that you can operate better in the world. But mental health also includes the 'softer' stuff: your emotions, thoughts and feelings, and your general sense of wellness.

Mental health can be impacted by everything you come into contact with: other people, your life experiences, your personal biology and tendencies, the choices you make, the food you eat and the lifestyle you design. Hopefully, this book will have given you some structure when it comes to the final point on that list, but if you find that other factors are impacting your mental health, it's always a good step to take protective action (check out the 'Resources' chapter for more information and suggestions).

One of the most important components, when it comes to dealing with your own mental wellbeing, is *awareness*. You can have all the support networks and structures and professional help available in the world, but if you're not able to perceive and then respond to your personal mental wellbeing, you might not be able to utilize it. The first step is always to notice. Then, from that perspective, you can choose how to respond.

Looking out for yourself

So, how to notice? One word of caution before we begin: an intuitive awareness of your own mental wellbeing takes *time* to build up. It takes time to build up the instinctive senses that enable you to respond to changes in your mood or emotions or wellbeing. It also often takes practice, and a sense of disciplined persistence.

165

Think about it like this: we get to have this human experience for quite a few decades, if we're lucky. That whole time, we're gathering information about ourselves and about the world; we're taking in new material; we're being educated through information and experience – every single day of our lives. If you're between the ages of 18 and 30, you actually haven't been present in your life for that long. Before 18, we're often preoccupied with finding our external place in the world, and it might not be until our 20s that we turn inwards, figuring out who we are and what we like and what we need to stay *well*. You are, of course, the author of your own existence – but it takes a little time to figure out the story.

On a practical level, then, what can you do to get started? I'd encourage you to explore your own mental health and wellbeing through the exercises in Chapters 3 and 4 – make it a part of your purpose-finding activities. After all, your purpose should be inextricably linked to a sense of mental wellbeing – it doesn't really make sense to go for a goal that doesn't align with your mental health, and you certainly don't want to sacrifice your mental health at the altar of external achievement. So, you can prioritize your own wellbeing by making it a fundamental part of your purpose-orientated strategy. Try setting it as one of your goals or ambitions, or write it into your mission statement, or set it out on your dream CV.

The other thing I'd encourage is creating an informal wellness check-in for yourself. In Appendix 2, I've included a template for a weekly wellness checklist – this is something I've used myself for a number of years, and I've found it to be incredibly useful when it comes to understanding myself over time. The power of the checklist practice – as I mentioned elsewhere in this book – lies in its consistency. Over time, completing regular checklists gives you an evolving sense of how your life is shaping up, and you can use that information to make decisions and choices accordingly. A regular checklist practice also has the benefit of giving you a sense of control and ownership over something – like mental health – that can seem a little incoherent, intangible or intimidating.

Knowing your rituals

We'll cover mental and physical rituals below, but to start, a few general thoughts. First, let's begin to reclaim the concept of wellness. We're constantly told that 'wellness' looks a certain way – maybe it involves long baths, or nice walks, or early nights. Maybe wellness is expensive – it might look like skin-care products or supplements or pricey fitness classes. Or it might just look totally unrealistic – cold showers at 5am, productivity hacks or extensive morning routines. But wellness is actually a basic concept, and it's worth redefining it before we go any further.

The basic definition of wellness is as follows: 'a state of good health, especially as an actively-pursued goal'. It doesn't set out what a state of good health necessarily has to look like – the most important thing is that your behaviours are aligned towards the 'good health' that you want. So, if (like me) 5am showers would make you feel cold, exhausted and demotivated, that's not *your* definition of wellness. The great thing about redefining the concept is that you get to choose your goal, according to your ideal state of good health, and then you can pick your favourite, most effective, most enjoyable routes to get you there.

Take a moment to write your own definition of wellness in a notebook or on a sheet of paper.

Now, using that definition, pick and choose a couple of favourite practices from the remainder of this chapter to form your definition of wellness. You might also, once you're done, like to return to Chapters 3 and 4, in order to integrate an element of wellness into your general purpose-finding work.

Meditation

An overview of meditation

Meditation is generally seen as the use of a technique (for example, visualization, breathwork or mindfulness) to obtain clarity of thought and peace of mind. Meditation has been around in various forms for thousands of years, so you're joining a long tradition when you begin to practise, but it's grown in popularity as our culture becomes more frantic and fast-paced. A simple meditation practice would be as follows:

Settle yourself in a comfortable position. It doesn't necessarily have to be a cross-legged 'meditation' position: you can just settle in a place in which the body feels alert but relaxed.

Close your eyes, if this feels comfortable – if not, take a 'soft' gaze (which means 'unfocusing' your attention and gazing at something, perhaps just a spot on the floor).

Bring your attention to your breath. Focus all of your awareness on the breath as you inhale and exhale. See if you can recognize all the details of the movement: focus on the texture of the breath, the pace, the depth, the intensity, etc.

When thoughts cross your mind (which they will, for the vast majority of people!), simply let them pass. You can 'observe' the thought as it passes, but the intention is not to engage with it – just let it move on. Repeat this process with each thought that comes into your mind.

After your meditation is complete (you could set yourself a timer for anywhere between five and 20 minutes, or just gently bring yourself out when you feel ready), you can open or refocus your eyes, stretch out your body and gently move back into your day.

You might like to pair this basic meditation practice with an intention-setting exercise or mantra (see Chapter 4).

For the more experienced

If you're an experienced meditator looking to integrate an element of purpose-finding work into your practice, you can easily bring your preferred style of practice into any of the exercises outlined in Chapters 3 and 4. For example, you can start and close a purpose-finding exercise with a brief meditation, or you could use an intention-setting meditation to guide your purpose work. If you get stuck for inspiration during the course of a purpose practice, or you feel overwhelmed, emotional or frustrated by any of the self-reflective exercises, you can turn to your meditation practice for support and connection.

Meditation practice is also a great time to check back in with your purpose-finding work, if you already have a regular routine set up. For example, if you meditate every morning or evening, you can remind yourself at this time of your current purpose, or your purpose for the day, or any goals and ambitions that came out of your purpose-driven work.

Note, however, that this is not about hoping that your purpose comes into existence as a result of meditation (this is more like the concept of 'manifestation', which is not covered in this book). Instead, you're using habit-stacking to link your purpose work to an existing routine. You can do the same thing by linking your purpose-finding work with habits like having your first cup of tea in the morning, or having a weekly clear-out of your desk, or the fresh start of a new month.

Mindfulness

An overview of mindfulness

Although the words 'mindfulness' and 'meditation' are often used interchangeably, they're actually distinct concepts. Mindfulness is often described as a particular type of meditation, and there are lots of other types of meditation (for example: vipassanā, chanting or body-scans). But, in my experience as a yoga and meditation teacher, it's often mindfulness that people are thinking of when they want to be more 'present' during their daily lives; more 'in the moment'. It's these same qualities of 'aliveness' that make mindfulness practice a great foundation for a purpose-driven life.

A basic definition of mindfulness is as follows:

Mindfulness is awareness that arises through paying attention, on purpose, in the present moment, non-judgmentally.[12]

Each element in the definition plays a distinct role in the practice of mindfulness.

- '*Awareness that arises through paying attention*': this breaks down the fundamental skill involved in practising mindfulness – the art of paying attention.
- '*On purpose*': this is the intentional part of the process, and it's what the *practice* of mindfulness is really about. Instead of a one-off achievement, mindfulness is intended to be an ongoing discipline.
- '*In the present moment*': this is the core of mindfulness teaching, and focuses the attention on the present moment. This is actually harder than you might think, especially if you're new to the practice. Most of the time, our minds default to the future or the past, and we're rarely fully present.
- '*Non-judgementally*': this (often overlooked) element is fundamental to a sustainable

---

[12] This is the definition used by Jon Kabat-Zinn, the founder of Mindfulness-Based Stress Reduction.

mindfulness practice. Whenever I teach mindfulness (especially if I'm teaching to a group of high-achieving, young professionals), I always encounter people who claim to have failed at mindfulness. There isn't really a way to fail: if you're practising, you're on the right path. This is the element of non-judgement that we should return to, as students of mindfulness, as many times as we need to.

Basic mindfulness practices

If you're interested in mindfulness and the many benefits it can bring, start small. Like any habit, mindfulness will be integrated into your life most effectively if you build up a practice, rather than jumping in with intimidating goals. You can also introduce your mindfulness practice into an existing habit – for example, taking a mindful shower or making a mindful cup of tea. The beauty of this type of mindfulness practice (sometimes referred to as 'mindful activities') is that you can really apply it to anything, so long as you're holding to the qualities we outlined above:

- awareness through paying attention;
- on purpose;
- in the present moment; and
- non-judgementally.

173

A more advanced mindfulness practice could involve a scheduled seated meditation practice (try 10–15 minutes to start with, once or twice a day), bringing the attention to the breath to begin with, and then focusing on the present moment. There are a lot of great resources available to help you build this practice, and you'll find some recommendations for books, podcasts and apps in the 'Resources' chapter.

Conversations

The importance of talking it out

This might sound obvious, but talking to other people is an often-overlooked part of your mental health strategy. Perhaps the reason it gets overlooked is that it doesn't have the same easy attraction as a wellness practice like 'candles and a good book', or perhaps it's because conversations with others are intimate and complex and often messy. As much as we'd like others to respond in the ways we want, it's rare that we get this type of perfect communication. Instead, we get another human, someone else with their own background and history and perspective, and things get complicated fairly fast. On the other hand, however, it's actually this aspect – the complexity of communication with another human – that makes it so important.

A couple of notes about mental health communication, first. If you ever feel like your problems would benefit from a qualified professional, trust your instinct. You don't have to have a mental health 'problem' to take this route, and there are a lot of resources available that make financial concerns less of an issue. Just like any important decision, make sure you do your research first – figure out what you want to talk about, or if there are any specific topics of interest, and then search for someone qualified in that area. If you don't feel aligned with your therapist, you can always look for another – this is your path, after all, and you're in control of who gets to support you on it.

Aside from therapy, you might turn to the people closest to you to talk about how things are going, and about your mental health in general. Again, choose the right person with intention – sometimes it's the case that your closest family or friends wouldn't understand, or they might be dealing with their own mental health struggles. So, give it a little thought – you can always raise the topic in a lighter way, seeing it as an opportunity to check in or catch up with the other person.

The art of empathy

Flipping the scenario above, it's possible that people close to you are wanting to talk about their own mental health, too. We're all walking our own paths, dealing with our own emotions and experiencing our own challenges. It might be that, with a little encouragement and an open, accepting environment, other people want to share their own journey with you as well. At a high level, some key principles to prepare for this kind of scenario are as follows:

- *Empathy*: this is generally defined as the ability to sense someone's emotions, or imagine what they might be feeling. Empathy is a skill, just like any other character trait, and you can develop it through active listening (see below) and then asking for confirmation of your understanding. It's possible to do this in a non-mechanical way, too – instead of simply listening and then repeating back your understanding, you can ask follow-up questions, get the other person to describe an experience, or suggest something that might be relatable and ask them for their views.

- *Active listening*: next time you're in a deep conversation with someone, observe how many times you want to interject. This includes times when you think you're being helpful or offering an interesting perspective. There are, of course, times to share your views, but see if you can also work on the skill of listening. The 'active' element of listening includes carefully taking in the information you gather and using it to formulate questions or perspectives.

- *The unspoken elements*: a significant amount of our communication is expressed before we've even said a word. From the posture we have, to the way we enter a room, to our stillness or activity level, to the way we make or break eye contact – all of these elements are saying something. If you're sitting down to listen to someone else, see if you can pick up on the subtleties of their non-verbal cues. Similarly, be aware that your own body language is saying something to them, however unconscious that process may be. So, if you're taking the role of listener, make sure you're appearing open, not intrusive, cold, intimidating or hostile. Go for relaxed, and as open as possible – but attentive.

For when you don't want to talk

Let's return to the definition of wellness. Remember that the key components of that definition are *good health* (as defined by you) and a *plan* to get towards it. Neither of those things is clear-cut, and it's not going to be a linear path to reach a utopian state of permanent wellness. Instead, your life, just like everyone else's, will move in seasons. Sometimes you'll want to talk, sometimes you won't. You're moving in a rhythm, after all – energy, rest, introversion: it's all part of the texture of life. And so, it's okay to encounter times when you don't want to talk about the things that are going on. The real skill is about *noticing*, and then choosing *how* you want to respond. This is the choice that gives you the power to design your life, and it's the fundamental message that lies at the heart of this book.

Your body

It probably won't surprise you, but the approach in this section is going to be consistent with the skill-set we've been working on so far. We'll cover the basics (most of which are far simpler than the wellness industry would like you to believe), and we'll approach it all using the awareness principle discussed above. In short, the key is to *observe* what's going on with your body, and develop an intuitive sense of *awareness* about what it feels like to inhabit your body. From that position, you can make informed decisions about what to do next.

Being embodied

One of the most important principles of this work – one closely aligned with self-awareness, meditation and spirituality – is the concept of embodiment. This is often described as filling something with life, or bringing something into a 'whole'. It's a great way to describe practices like yoga, dance or other immersive movement – the idea that you practise the sensation of embodiment in these specific contexts, at these specific times, and then you're able to experience this sensation in a more consistent way in the rest of your life.

Without going into a huge amount of detail, philosophy or scientific understanding on the topic of embodiment (see the 'Resources' chapter for suggestions on where to dive in deeper), here are a couple of high-level thoughts as you develop your practice.

Embodiment is often discouraged, and it can be uncomfortable to engage with

For those of us immersed in Western-capitalist culture, embodiment isn't often encouraged. From the 'diet mentality' to unattainable aesthetic ideals, we're often pushed in the direction of control and restriction. We're encouraged to 'achieve' a body that society finds acceptable, or desirable, or (in a newer iteration of body-focused advertising) to extend our lifespan regardless of the consequences. Obviously, being at home in your body and comfortable with yourself doesn't sell as well as a sense of perpetual discomfort. It's clear, then, that embodiment isn't usually embraced in mainstream culture (of course, things are changing rapidly, and diversity and unconditional acceptance is – finally – much more visible in recent years).

So, in order to practise embodiment – for example, through yoga or body-focused meditation – there might be a necessary element of rebellion against the dominant culture. There also might be a little rebellion against *yourself* – if you've grown up in a certain way, with a certain perspective about your body, you might encounter difficulty when it comes to fully inhabiting your body. As with all of the practices in this book, it takes time. We're thinking *years* here, rather than *months* or *weeks*. And it's certainly not a quick-fix, five-step plan to permanent success (regardless of how well that would sell). Instead, this is a slow, gentle process of getting to know yourself and starting to make peace with being a human being inside of a human body. We'll cover some more specific practices in the remainder of this chapter, but – to return to the principles in the introduction of this chapter – the main idea is that *you are a whole person – mind, body and self.*

Movement

There are as many different ways of moving your body as there are people on the earth, so whatever expression you give to your movement will be individual to you. Just like the strategies for dealing with your mental health: choose something that you enjoy, something that makes you feel engaged and present, and then keep some consistency going over a period of weeks. After that, see how you feel, and reassess – maybe switch up your practice, or take a break, or continue as you were, or step up your energy level. This all comes from that sense of intuitive, instinctive understanding of yourself and your life, the same sense we've been developing throughout this book.

A couple of ideas:

- In my experience as a fitness instructor, people get into movement best when they fit it into their existing lifestyle, rather than changing their whole lifestyle to fit the movement. For me, this has always played out in terms of timing – I've never been productive or energetic in the mornings, so an evening yoga or ballet class has always worked best for me. You might be the opposite, so try a few things out and see what you like.

- Another thing that puts people off bringing more movement into their lives is the strictness or intensity of some fitness programmes. To start inhabiting your body, and moving in a way that feels good, begin as small as you want. If you're working from home, this could be a stretch sequence in-between sessions at your desk. Or, it could look like an early evening run, or a dance class with friends. It might look like a sport or a physical hobby, like hiking or walking or swimming. It might even look like a blend of all of these activities.

When I approach my own movement practice, I try to start with the question:

What is it that I feel like doing today?
What would serve my body and my mind?

Note that there are always two elements you're dealing with: the body and the mind. Although we're developing an intuitive, embodied sense of movement, we also have to handle the demands and desires of the mind. Just like the meditation techniques above, the most effective strategy is often to acknowledge and observe thoughts, before deciding how to react to them. Here's an example:

Let's say you had a slow day yesterday, and your mind is telling you to get back on track. After taking a brief embodiment check-in, you realize you're actually still exhausted. There are a lot of ways you could proceed – for example:

1. push through with the workout, listen to your mind and stick to a predetermined plan;
2. listen to your physical exhaustion, honour the sensations in your body and take a break; or

3. give it a little time, check in a couple of hours later and see if you have any more clarity.

There are lots of different options here, and no right or wrong way to approach it. With the list above, it might be that you decide to push through and feel better afterwards. Or, you might push through and wish you'd rested. Or, you might defer the decision to a later time and still feel undecided. The only philosophy I'm advocating here is that of *awareness*, and then an intentional *choice* of reaction. Just as for your purpose-orientated work, you're the designer of your own existence. You can gather the information, pause, listen to your life, and then choose how you want to proceed.

Nutrition

The intuitive approach applies here, as well. The resources section is full of intuitive eating recommendations, so this section will be brief. Just a couple of things to note:

- Taking care of your own nutrition can be seen through the same perspective we've applied to the other elements of this book. At the core of the intuitive eating approach is the skill of being embodied – of being fully connected to what it feels like to be alive, and making decisions in accordance with that.

- The same 'counter-cultural' element we touched on above applies here, too. When it comes to the idealized expectations of the wellness industry, you can see the same factors at play when it comes to choosing the food we eat (or don't eat). As with the sections above, I'd encourage you to take a personalized approach here – define what it means to you to have 'good health' when it comes to nutrition, and then educate yourself about the best, most enjoyable ways to get there. I'd also encourage an approach that focuses less on right and wrong, and more on what it actually feels like to be alive – to feed yourself well; to enjoy being in your body; to care for yourself like you'd care for someone you love.

- Finally, the principle of *neutrality* (covered above, under the mental health discussion) also applies. It's much easier to sell products by labelling something a 'treat', or demonizing certain foods as 'bad', than it is to accept the fact that *food is food*. In itself, it's neutral of morality: it's not negative or positive. It's just a question of how things make you feel, and the choices you make based on that information. You'll find much more on all of this in the 'Resources' chapter.

Sleep

I used to suffer with insomnia when I was younger – not so bad that it became harmful, but bad enough that it was a pretty frequent concern. I remember trying everything – careful bedtime routines, structuring my day around my sleep – but it wasn't until I let go of the idea of controlling the process that I actually was able to recover from it. Put simply, I gave up on trying to make 'sleep' happen. Instead, I started to trust my body to get the sleep it needed, reassuring myself that I could always make up for lost sleep in the following nights.

Obviously, this approach doesn't apply if you're dealing with other factors (anxiety, medical conditions, etc.) – I'd always recommend reaching out to a GP or sleep specialist, in those cases. But you might find that the intuitive approach helps from a psychological perspective – take the pressure off, observe your body and your mind, and allow things to happen. Less pressurized control, more awareness, and then you can choose what to do from there.

A few final thoughts

Boundaries

One of the most helpful practices for organizing my life has been *boundaries*. Boundaries can give you structure and form: they let other people know when it's okay to step closer, and when it's not. They can also mark out periods of time – boundaries around your focused working hours; boundaries around your periods of rest and play; boundaries around the things that matter most to you, so you can make sure they're protected.

It's difficult to set boundaries for a variety of reasons. People may not recognize or respect your boundaries (this might especially be the case with close friends or family members, and *especially* if setting boundaries is new for you). And in a work environment, you might not have much choice about where your boundaries fall (for example, if you're in a junior role).

My hope is that you can use the principles of this book and apply them to boundary-setting. If you can gather information from your purpose-finding work in Chapters 3 and 4, you can make informed decisions about boundaries when it comes to your career or your work in the world. Armed with a clearer vision of what really matters, you can start to decide: where should I allocate my time? What should get priority, and when? How should I choose to structure my life, despite the various demands that are placed on me?

When it comes to personal boundary-setting, this might take a little more assertion. I'd recommend using the tools on mental health to check in with yourself – see how you're really feeling, and make decisions in alignment with that. Boundaries can always be temporary: if you feel like you need space, claim it for yourself. Open communication and empathy towards other people's feelings is helpful here, too – but remember that the primary purpose of your boundaries is to protect you on a personal level, so maintain the position that makes you feel most safe.

Balance

I don't know if a perfect 'life' balance exists. Instead, I like to think of it as 'integration' – the inextricable blend of your work and your life and your passions and your networks and your wellbeing and your *purpose*. Integration is everything all wrapped up into one vibrant, complex creation. Go towards the things you care most about; the people you want to keep around; the places you feel at home in; the body and the mental space you know reflects your idea of wellness. Go towards the life you want to design – intentional architecture, based on a lifetime of experience. You get to choose, after all – so you can decide what balance is for yourself.

Being human

One final note, to finish our work here. We're probably not getting any of this right on the first try. In fact, there's no idea of 'right' that we're aiming to reach

187

anyway. Instead, we're on a slow mission to become more fully alive, and to redesign our lives around the purpose we're figuring out for ourselves. I'm not sure if we ever really need to find a final, perfect answer – the journey is really the point.

Remember that pilgrimage idea we started out with? A pilgrimage is a slow, spiritual process – you're supposed to savour the steps you take, rather than rush through and reach the destination. Maybe our generation has lost this sense of slowness, of taking time to reach a place that really matters. Our culture rewards quick-fixes and short-cuts and how-to manuals. If you've got this far, I'm hoping that you'll understand that this book is not intended to give you the answers. Instead, it's a starting point – a map and a guide and a compass to point you in the right direction.

The rest? Well, that's yours to design.

CHAPTER 8

FREQUENTLY ASKED QUESTIONS

Everything you need to know going forwards

In this chapter, we'll cover some of the most frequently asked questions when it comes to navigating your sense of purpose. For more resources, guidance and next steps (including how you can continue this work, or ask me questions directly), head over to the 'Resources' chapter.

What happens if my purpose changes over time?

Congratulations: you're human. Most (if not all) of us will experience changes in our purpose, mission and passions during the course of our lives. Very few people find a singular purpose at a very young age and carry it all the way through to the end. It's possible, of course, but examples like this tend to reflect a high-level purpose – something broad, like 'giving back', or 'helping others', rather than a definition of purpose that focuses on specific details.

For the rest of us, we'll find that life moves in seasons. There will be times when our purpose seems clear and attainable, and times when we feel totally off track. There will be times when we push forwards and learn about ourselves and see the path ahead, and times when we step back, listen carefully, and wait to figure out our next move. The consistent part about this whole process, though, is the *intention* to work towards your idea of purpose – however you conceptualize it, and whatever it means for you in your particular season of life. This sense of intention is the element that leads to a purpose-orientated existence.

What happens if I don't want to do the work for a while?

We don't always have to be fully focused on self-development, and purpose-focused work can be tiring. Just like any other practice in your life, it's fine to pause. A couple of thoughts, as you decide to take your break:

- Try to make any decision to step back with awareness. Deciding to step back from personal development deliberately is often a good choice, if you feel you need it. But stepping back through complacency, apathy or overwhelm can be a warning sign, rather than a self-care initiative. If you feel like you're having to take a break from your life because it just seems too much to handle, it might be a good idea to re-evaluate, and/or speak to someone about it.

- Relatedly, stepping back from purpose-finding work is a great time to step *up* your foundational wellness practices. If you're taking a break to slow down, you might find it helpful to check in with your body and mind – see where you're at, and start to strengthen the foundations that will enable you to return, when you're ready, with a sense of new energy.

- Sometimes, this kind of work – for example, mapping out your past experiences – can be difficult for other reasons. Perhaps it feels stressful to reflect on the past, or perhaps you just don't want to address certain aspects of your life. There's nothing in this work that compels you to do things a certain way – the benefit of the approach in this book is that you can pick and choose your favourite practices. You can also redesign the practices, using the frameworks suggested, to create something that works for you. (If there is something in

191

your life that feels like a significant block to self-development, or an issue that you feel would benefit from some assistance, it might be a good idea to speak to someone about it.)

What if I can't figure out the answers?

Luckily, there's no way you can fail at this work. We're entering a space where you're free to create, without fear of accidentally picking the wrong path or making the wrong decision. This work responds to you and your life – you can *always* revisit, rewrite and redesign. Test out your plans in reality, and check in with yourself to see whether they're working for you. Think of yourself less as a performer, needing to get things perfect to please an external audience, and more as a choreographer – designing steps to see if they work, and redesigning if you don't feel satisfied or comfortable with them.

These are big topics, and most of us haven't ever encountered them before, unless we've been through therapy or engaged in other existential or spiritual training. It's totally understandable if it feels over-whelming to really *look* at our lives. The key is to come at the work from a position of neutrality – not judging anything you learn about yourself or your life, and seeing it as an information-gathering exercise, rather than a test. It's an unusual perspective to prac-tice, especially in a society that generally focuses on external achievement to the exclusion of everything else – but there's no grade at the end of this process, no presentation, and no certificate. Just you, your life, and your ever-evolving sense of purpose.

Is it too late for me to do the work?

In my opinion, there's no cut-off point to this work. Although these existential questions of meaning and purpose become more pronounced or urgent as we move through big life transitions (approaching adulthood, choosing our first careers, switching jobs, retirement and other significant life events), there's no 'end' point at which it becomes irrelevant. You *always* have the opportunity to choose your path, within the context in which you find yourself. This applies whether you're nine years old or 99 years old. The biggest questions of life don't ever get any less important.

And, remember – there's no end goal. Even if you do start the work at nine years old, you'll probably still be revisiting and reworking the same questions at 99. This is the real gift of being alive: the ability to discover ourselves again and again and again.

What if I don't have the energy or motivation for the work?

The world can be exhausting. Between careers and families and relationships and socializing and exercising and posting on social media, we barely have a second to catch our breath, let alone delve into this kind of work. Right?

Well, yes – but this might be part of the problem. We're encouraged to move fast through the world, constructing our lives according to predetermined plans and achieving things to impress others, and we rarely stop and question *why* we're actually doing it. And, importantly, whether the choices we carry out on auto-pilot are actually the ones we'd design for ourselves, if we sat down with a blank piece of paper and a spare hour or two. The risk is, of course, that we wake up one Monday morning a decade later, and wonder how we ended up there, and where all the time went.

My intention with this book is to make purpose-finding work both *accessible* and *practical*. By splitting up the exercises separately, and giving you the ability to pick and choose from a selection of options, it might be easier to carve out time when you can find it. And by indicating how long each exercise might take, it might make it easier to pick the ones that work with your schedule. A word of caution, though – these exercises are most effective if you can bring a level of awareness and attention to them. Twenty minutes spent in full concentration on an exercise is likely to be more effective than an hour multitasking your way through it.

One practical strategy is to see this work as an important part of your self-care routine. Realistically, this might mean replacing something else that you currently do, but it doesn't have to be a dramatic invest-ment of time. I'd also encourage you to *enjoy* working through the practices – design yourself a ritual that you look forward to (for example, making your favourite drink, turning your phone on silent and finding a quiet space to reflect – or whatever else works for you).

Remember, too, that this work will spill over and impact other areas of your life, so it's never just a one-time input of energy. Instead, it's more like an investment – make an initial payment of time, and you'll find the benefits return to you, with regularity, over the following weeks and months.

What happens if I just want to start again?

It can feel scary to start again. Sometimes it feels like time was wasted, or like you have to let go of every-thing that came before. There's an element of grief in this process; of mourning the vision of a life you imagined, one that doesn't really fit with the way your actual life is evolving. Sometimes starting again isn't your choice, either. Whether it's a break-up, or an unexpected loss, or a change of direction that was forced on you – sometimes, we're faced with the bleak reality that our life isn't headed the way we want.

I recognize this feeling, because I've been through it myself. And, in fact, the purpose-focused work from this book has often been my guide in those moments.

It's given me the ability to reclaim autonomy and control over the elements of my life that I'd given up to someone else, or to something else. It enabled me to reconnect with myself, in a way that was sometimes difficult and sad, and always ultimately rewarding. It gave me a vision for the path ahead, and it provided the tools with which to design a life I wanted to live – even if it wasn't the one I'd previously envisaged.

There are countless ways to create a life. Sometimes we have a vision and execute it; sometimes we're handed a new blank page when we thought we were about to finish a masterpiece. But either way, we're creators, choosing to respond to the circumstances of our lives with intention and integrity.

In the end, life presents itself to every single one of us, and asks, simply: what next?

CHAPTER 9

SOME INSPIRATION

Thoughts from a few purpose-led individuals, to inspire your own journey

As we've explored in this book, purpose looks different for everyone, and it plays a different role in each individual life. Below is a collection of thoughts about purpose from people who have inspired me on my own journey.

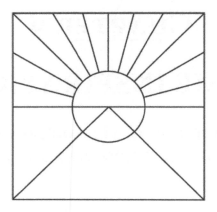

Sarah Malcolm

Sarah is a London-based teacher, podcaster and all-round wellness inspiration. After discovering yoga at university, she has used the practice over many years as a way to explore embodiment and live mindfully. Through her classes and her podcast, Sarah has cultivated a welcoming, holistic community.

Sarah and I met on yoga teacher training, and have practised together in classes and on retreats over many years. Above all, it's Sarah's blend of light-hearted attitude and depth of character that continues to inspire me.

What 'purpose' means to Sarah:

My current purpose is to find contentment in the ordinary. To appreciate the things I had perhaps been taking for granted, like the first sip of coffee in the morning or a moment of uncontrollable laughter with my partner. My purpose is to simply be and acknowledge the power in that. Truthfully, I could say a thousand different things about what my purpose is, but feeling content will always feel the most honest. And reminding myself of that allows me to work in a kinder way.

Find Sarah here:

Her website: https://sarahmalcolm.co.uk/
Her Instagram: www.instagram.com/sarahmalcs/
Her podcast: https://sarahmalcolm.co.uk/podcast/

Karis Scarlette

Karis is a dancer, teacher and coach who began her classical ballet training at the age of two. After training at the Royal Ballet School, she overcame a devastating injury and started a career as an international teacher. Now a leader in the adult ballet community, Karis also focuses on meditation and holistic wellbeing. I took my first class with Karis many years ago, and have been inspired by her energy, passion and elegance ever since.

What 'purpose' means to Karis:

To find your purpose means you've aligned physically and emotionally with your soul's calling, with what you're supposed to be doing in life. To have a purpose means taking responsibility for your energy and actions in order to create the life you want.

Find Karis here:

Her website: www.karisscarlette.com/
Her Instagram: www.instagram.com/karisscarlette/

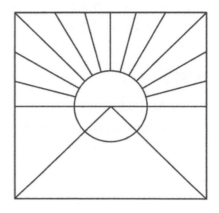

Merritt Moore

Dr. Merritt Moore graduated with Magna Cum Laude Honors in Physics from Harvard and graduated with a PhD in Atomic and Laser Physics from the University of Oxford. She also pursues a professional ballet career, previously with the Zurich Ballet, Boston Ballet, English National Ballet, and Norwegian National Ballet. She was named on the Forbes 30 Under 30 list, and was one of the 12 selected candidates to undergo rigorous astronaut selection on BBC Two's 'Astronauts: Do you have what it takes?'.

This blend of abilities – across the arts and the sciences – is incredibly rare, and Merritt's long list of achievements is a demonstration of her talent. For me, it's the mix of passion and intelligence that is so inspiring: the capacity to integrate skills from different disciplines to create something entirely unique.

What 'purpose' means to Merritt:

My drive and passion came at 17 years old. My dad handed me a blank piece of paper and pen and said 'write down what would make you super excited to work towards, and most importantly, write down why that dream would help others'. This was at a time when I had lost all motivation and hope. I was pursuing physics and ballet and because I had started both so late, I was told I would never make it in either. Focusing my purpose on others is what has given me endless energy in everything that I do.

Find Merritt here:

Her website: http://physicsonpointe.com/
Her Instagram: www.instagram.com/physicsonpointe/

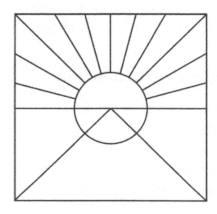

Katy Hirst

Katy is an ordinand at Ridley Hall, Cambridge. She is also a blogger, speaker and leader, blending traditional ways of life with modern values and principles. Katy and I met on a monastic training programme, as part of an initiative established by the Archbishop of Canterbury. As well as her warm, welcoming nature, Katy's intelligence and commitment always stood out to me. It takes strength of character to commit to a different, counter-cultural way of life, and Katy's personality reflects that.

What 'purpose' means to Katy:

Over the last few years, my idea of purpose has shifted. It used to be about success and achievement – doing the best that I was able to do in the most impressive way. But now, my sense of purpose is about being fully who I was created to be, no more and no less. Rather than my 'best' self, I'm more interested in my 'true' self, which includes limits, incapacities and finitude.

Concretely, at the moment this means following my calling to be a priest in the Anglican Church, for which I am now in training. It's not glamorous or impressive, there are no clear metrics of success, but I experience more peace and joy now than ever before. I am doing the thing for which God made me, and doing so in the knowledge that my main purpose is this spiritual relationship, which no amount of success or failure can change.

Find Katy here:

Her website: https://katyhirst.com/
Her Twitter: https://twitter.com/katyhirst

Stef Sword-Williams

Stefanie Sword-Williams is the founder and author of *F*ck Being Humble* (a platform set up to encourage individuals to be unapologetically proud of their achievements and overcome the fear of self-promotion). Stef was named on the Forbes 30 Under 30 list and has delivered a TEDx talk focused on why we need to be less humble. She leads courses and delivers workshops to a wide, diverse audience.

Stef has an exceptional ability to deliver an important message with a grounded, light-hearted attitude. *F*ck Being Humble* is not just a business or a book, but also a manifesto for a new generation of leaders, and Stef has crafted the message with expertise.

What 'purpose' means to Stef:

I think my purpose is definitely rooted in story-telling for good, supporting people and opening up new opportunities to inspire others. When we look at the definition of a 'brand purpose' we would define it as the reason that company or business exists. So, if we look at the definition on an individual level, it's about understanding why you are here, what you can positively contribute to, and knowing where you get the most sense of enjoyment in life.

I feel lucky to have combined my purpose and career so early on in my journey, so if I could recommend one thing to anyone reading this it's to not let your purpose be defined by what you think you *should* be doing or what is *expected* of you. You'll only be truly content when you choose a purpose that suits your needs and the life you want to live.

Find Stef here:

Her website: www.fuckbeinghumble.com/
Her Instagram: www.instagram.com/stefaniesw/

Danielle Copperman

Danielle Copperman is a model, writer, author and entrepreneur. She is passionate about inspiring others to adopt more holistic habits in life, and promotes sustainability, wellbeing and self-care. Danielle's talents extend across so many different disciplines, but her message – of living well, and taking care of yourself and your environment – is a powerful and enduring theme. In a world of influencers and competing narratives, Danielle stands out with an educated, thoughtful perspective.

What 'purpose' means to Danielle:

> To me, purpose means having an intention and integrity behind what you're doing. I know

first-hand that doing something for the sake of it, because other people are doing it, or because you think you should be doing it, doesn't end well. It generally doesn't feel authentic, easeful or enjoyable. Doing something with purpose is about bringing an element of passion and determination into the equation, and reason – meaning – for what and how you do something.

For me, purpose means doing something worthy, to support someone or something, to initiate change or to improve something in some way. Purpose is about doing something not just for fun, but doing something for a real reason, and having purpose drives projects much more steadily and sturdily. It is the root, the foundations, of something. It brings undying motivation and determination, and helps you to feel committed and a part of something bigger than yourself.

Whatever your purpose is, it is usually something that underpins everything you do in life, not just career or one area of your life. Having a purpose starts as something personal, and is weaved into everything you do in a consistent and sustainable way that feels good, and goes further.

Find Danielle here:

Her website: https://daniellecopperman.com/homepage
Her Instagram: www.instagram.com/dcopperman/
Her podcast: www.theprocess.life/podcast

RESOURCES

A few recommendations

Books

For your mind:

- *The Miracle of Mindfulness* – Thich Nhat Hanh
- *Wherever You Go, There You Are* – Jon Kabat-Zinn
- *Real Happiness* – Sharon Salzberg
- *F*ck Being Humble* – Stef Sword-Williams

For your body:

- *Well Being* – Danielle Copperman
- *The Body Keeps the Score* – Bessel Van Der Kolk
- *Train Happy* – Tally Rye
- *The F*ck It Diet* – Caroline Dooner

For your soul:

- *Man's Search for Meaning* – Viktor Frankl

- *Yes to Life, in Spite of Everything* – Viktor Frankl
- *Ikigai* – Hector Garcia
- *Letters from a Stoic* – Seneca
- Anything by Sartre, Camus or Kierkegaard

On race, class and privilege:

- *Natives: Race and Class in the Ruins of Empire* – Akala
- *Me and White Supremacy* – Layla F. Saad
- *The Class Ceiling* – Sam Friedman

Podcasts

For your mind:

- *How to Fail* – Elizabeth Day
- *The Fundamentalists* – Pete Rollins and Elliott Morgan
- *Hello Monday* – LinkedIn
- *Ten Percent Happier* – Dan Harris
- *The Knowledge Project* – Shane Parrish

For your body:

- *Kitchen Club* – Sarah Malcolm and Serena Louth

- *The F*ck It Diet* – Caroline Dooner

For your soul:

- *The Process* – Danielle Copperman
- *The Robcast* – Rob Bell
- *Under the Skin* – Russell Brand
- *Becoming Wise/On Being* – Krista Tippett

On social issues:

- *About Race* – Reni Eddo-Lodge
- *Reasons to be Cheerful* – Ed Miliband and Geoff Lloyd
- *Ear Hustle* – Radiotopia

Newsletters and blogs

- *Farnam Street* – Shane Parrish
- *Conversations on Love* – Natasha Lunn
- *Brain Pickings* – Maria Popova
- *Seth's Blog* – Seth Godin
- *Art of Gathering* – Priya Parker
- *School of Life* newsletter and blog
- *Rescue Time* blog

Organizations

Career Ready UK

Career Ready is a national charity with a mission to boost social mobility by empowering young people and giving their talents a platform to flourish. Career Ready work with young people, schools and colleges who face barriers in education and employment which cause their talents to often go undiscovered. A portion of the proceeds of this book will be donated to Career Ready.

Some other organizations to check out:

- Inspiring The Future
- Young Women's Trust
- NCVO / Charity Job
- Volunteering Matters
- Volunteer Match
- Red Cross

APPENDIX 1

A checklist of values

- Mastery
- Pleasure
- Freedom
- Openness
- Authenticity
- Growth
- Giving
- Balance
- Honesty
- Integrity
- Attention to detail
- Challenge
- Creativity
- Reputation
- Collaboration
- Independence
- Community
- Influence
- Security
- Flexibility
- Affluence

- Competition
- Innovation
- Self-awareness
- Consistency
- Solitude
- Spirituality
- Intellect
- Structure
- Fluidity
- Diversity
- Inclusion
- Leadership
- Wisdom
- Learning
- Equality
- Teamwork
- Experimentation
- Loyalty
- Faith
- Curiosity
- Humility

APPENDIX 2

A weekly wellness checklist

1. Reflect on the [day/week] that's just passed. If you could sum it up in three words, what would you say?

- No rules here, just the first things that come to mind as you reflect. Try and stick to single words: it can be pretty insightful to do the work of capturing your experience in the briefest format possible.

2. How are you doing on a physical level? Give yourself a mark out of ten for the following:

- spending some time outside (aim for at least 15 minutes) every day;
- eating well, at regular intervals (i.e. not consistently working through mealtimes or breaks);
- making an effort to stay hydrated throughout the day;

- incorporating some movement into your week – in whatever way feels best for you (gym, sports, dance, fitness classes…);
- getting enough sleep (most people need 7–9 hours a night, but adjust according to what feels good for you); and
- sitting (or standing) at your desk with good posture.

3. How's your mind doing? Give yourself a mark out of ten for the following:

- making progress towards goals or ambitions, whether in work or out of it;
- feeling like you supported others or contributed to your community;
- getting involved; feeling like you're doing meaningful work;
- finding genuine enjoyment in something each day (and taking the time to appreciate it); and
- catching up with colleagues, friends and family. Have you had a couple of decent (non-work) conversations with people that matter to you?

4. What about the bigger picture: meaning, purpose and mission?

It's worth reminding yourself of the fundamentals: why do you do the work you've chosen to do? What is it about your everyday life that gives you meaning? How do you find a sense of purpose in everyday life?

Even if you've been through these questions and answered them before, it's helpful to keep checking back in. And – of course – don't be nervous of changing the answers to the questions as your life evolves. The aim is simply to be as honest with yourself as possible.

5. Lastly, what are the three things you'd like to take forwards into your new week?

Using the answers to the questions above, make a quick list of three things you'd like to carry forwards to work on. It could be anything – from drinking more water, to setting up a conversation with your boss about career prospects. And it's not intended to be prescriptive, or another standard to measure yourself against. Instead, let it just be a simple intention-setting exercise: an opportunity to figure out where you'd like to go, and to map the steps to get there.

As you finish...

- Make a note of anything practical that came out of the exercise. Perhaps there's someone you need to get in touch with, or a new habit to track – if you need to carry over notes to your to-do list or calendar, do it now.

- Give yourself some space: try to avoid jumping straight back into work. Maybe take a walk, or get some fresh air. If more thoughts or ideas come, you can always add more detail to your checklist.
- If you have time, and if you've made the checklist a consistent habit, it's worth reviewing your previous weeks. Can you see where things seem to be headed? Is there an overall sense of purpose and development? If not, can you create one? It's your life, after all – it's worth taking the time to shape it with intention.

THE
PURPOSE
WORKSHOP

If you want to explore the topics of this book in more detail, or find ongoing support and community – you're in the right place.

Welcome to The Purpose Workshop.

We are a social impact business with a singular focus: to help you redesign your life. Our work is focused on navigating the topic of purpose, and we'll be your guide as you figure it out.

We offer three main products:

1. **Workshops** (self-paced online workshops, which you can complete anywhere, at any time);
2. **Resources** (workbooks and checklists); and
3. **An app** (community, wellness, fitness & personal development).

– **Find out more:**
   www.thepurposeworkshop.uk

– **Or connect with us on Instagram:**
   www.instagram.com/thepurposeworkshop

DEDICATIONS

To my parents and grandparents, for teaching me to chase my dreams. And to my brother, whose natural sense of purpose has been an inspiration in finding my own.

All images by Amy Patsalides (Brand Designer).

With endless thanks to Alison Jones and her team for bringing this book into reality!